Hidden Scotland

Hidden Scotland

Ann Lindsay

BIRLINN

This edition published in 2006 by
Birlinn Limited
West Newington House
10 Newington Road
Edinburgh
EH9 1QS

www.birlinn.co.uk

Reprinted 2010

First edition published in 1992 by Lochar Publishing, Moffat, Scotland
Copyright © Ann Lindsay 1992 and 2006

ISBN10: 1 84158 348 0
ISBN13: 978 1 84158 348 8

British Library Cataloguing-in-Publication Data
A catalogue record for this book is available from the British Library

Typeset by IMH(Cartrif), Loanhead, Scotland
Printed and bound by MPG Books Ltd, Bodmin

Contents

Acknowledgements

Author Acknowledgements

I would like to thank the following:

the *Scots Magazine*, within whose pages many of these tales, written by myself, first appeared;

Mrs Sheena Carmichael of Ford, Argyll, for all her information about Poltalloch, where she spent her childhood, and also sending me off to Kilneuair, which I would never have found without her exact directions;

Michael Davis for freely giving of his detailed research and writing on the Malcolms of Poltalloch, Argyll;

Thomas Kirk of Cardenden, Fife, for photos, tales and youthful memories of Willie Maclaren, artist;

Eleanor Harris of Argyll and Bute Local Studies, Dunoon;

Ian Thomson Cartwright of Robert Thomson's Craftsmen Ltd at Kilburn, York;

Douglas Kynoch of Aberdeen for photos and first-hand reminiscences of his grandfather, the sculptor Robert Morrison;

Murdo Morrison for information about the Whalebone Arch at his house in Lewis;

Allan Joyce of Lairg for adding a mysterious slant on the sinking of the HMS *Hampshire*;

John Ridgway of Ardmore, for his photo of the *English Rose III*, in which he and Chay Blyth had rowed across the Atlantic in 1966;

Ian Dale, Angus Weavers, based at House of Dun, by Montrose;

Paisley Museum Staff;

Suzann Barr of the Abriachan Forest Trust, near Inverness;

Nicola Taylor of the Gairloch Heritage Centre, Ross-shire;

Charles Currie of the National Trust for Scotland (North), for the background to the bridge over the Corrieshalloch Gorge, near Ullapool;

David Mackie of the Orkney Library and Archives;

Robin Mitchell of the Witchery Tours, Edinburgh;

Mrs Joan Johnson of Delgatie Castle, Turriff, for her tales about Captain Hay of Delgatie Castle, and her scones;

Bob Thomson of Coldingham, in the Borders;

the Aberlour Child Care Trust of Stirling;

Tony Scherr of Harris for all the background to Christ Church, on the Island of Ensay;

and the staff at Birlinn for assistance in piecing together all these hidden tales.

Picture Acknowledgements

Images on the following pages are reproduced by permission. All other images are from the author's private collection.

p6	Ian Dale, Angus weavers
p8	Van Werminick Photographers, Montrose
p25	Murdo Morrison, Glasgow
p56, p57	Gairloch Heritage Museum
p61, p62	Tom Kirk, Cardenden
p70	Kirkcaldy Museum
p74	Douglas Kynoch, Aberdeen
p76, p77	Bob Thomson, Coldingham
p82	Tweeddale Museum, Peebles
p86	Tony Scherr, Harris
p126, p127, p128	Aberlour Child Care Trust, Stirling
p172	Orkney Library and Archive
p181	John Ridgway, Ardmore
p208	Mrs Sheena Carmichael, Ford, Argyll

Map ix

Introduction

From the heart of her major cities to the middle of her moorlands and mountains, there are little-known and curious delights hidden throughout Scotland, from poignant graffiti on far-flung island crofts to tongue-in-cheek book titles within one of the most extravagant castles in Scotland. This book uncovers them.

Scotland is chock-full of the unexpected, the off-peak, the quirky, the amusing, full of truth or based merely on superstition and legend. This book delves into the lost and almost forgotten backyard of Scotland. Rushing past on trains or roads, walking or cycling over tracks and moor, we can fail to notice it, unless we know just where to look. This book reveals curious places, their stories and the people behind the tales. Perfectly ordinary buildings, unremarkable moorlands, ruined hamlets, curious, abandoned blocks of stones hide secret stories: from a lost Moroccan empress who turned out to be a headstrong red-haired lassie from Perthshire to hens housed secretly in caves; from gun emplacements and relics from Scotland's secret war efforts to ruined medieval churches which hide tales from the very cusp of the arrival of Protestantism; from wooden boats which ended up as roofs to Pictish stones and Arthurian grave mounds, all hidden from prying eyes.

There are whitewashed west-coast farms which housed and trained eighteenth-century 'heather priests', gleaming black furniture carved from Fife coal, fishing bothies for salmon netting on the Tay, doocots littering the countryside, ruined but still housing pigeons who recognise an ideal home when they see it, tide mills and curious circular cuttings in the Fife seaside rocks, used as a template for lighthouses. Times of war, even in the twentieth century, produced tales from remote areas, from places of refuge and replenishment for First World War U-boats – a cheque in payment might still be in the post to some luckless farmer – to gathering places for Atlantic convoys. Wooden wifies and truly royal queens crop up in unexpected places, achieving status simply by outliving their contemporaries or by landing in Moorish countries by mistake.

So many of Scotland's hidden gems were commonplace just a century or so ago, have often given their name to the hamlet or town, and are now forgotten. Others were so secret they never revealed themselves until stumbled across by accident. There is scarcely a mile in Scotland which does not hide some tale, and although in this journey round Scotland you tread on secrets aplenty, there are without doubt many, many more to search out.

This is no ordinary guide to what's on and where, at what price, at what opening times in Scotland. No general tourist tome is this. You can take this book in hand and seek out lost places, or curl up in the armchair and dream. But watch out! Just as today's newspaper is the stuff of tomorrow's archives, so today's familiar places might well be tomorrow's hidden Scotland.

Woven stories and fashionable tales

Flax, a very fickle trade

'Lint mills' and 'retting ponds', 'heckles' and 'scutch mills'; these words sound like nonsense nowadays but were once part of the everyday vocabulary of all country Scots. From the lowliest cottar houses supplying material to the largest manufacturers, flax growing and linen weaving, once commonplace activities, have almost died out. It is a totally vanished way of life, though one which has left a legacy of unexpected names. For example, lint gave its name to birds: linnets were popularly called 'linties'. And hecklers used to comb out flax fibres: nowadays they tease indiscretions out of politicians.

Flax has been cultivated in Britain since at least the Bronze Age. It is also one of the very earliest known agricultural crops, cultivated from Western Asia to Europe, later grown virtually worldwide. This is partly owing to the amazing tolerance and adaptability of the flax seed itself, which will grow in a variety of soils and climates and at many altitudes.

The heyday of the flax plant in Scotland was the eighteenth century, when flax growing was developed into a substantial industry, aided by the government. Many local lairds set up flax mills, or lint mills as they were called, and by the 1790s there were few parishes in Scotland where flax was not grown, even in the northern islands.

After this high spot in production, the story of flax is one of long but steady decline. During the Second World War there was a brief revival, and during the early 1970s and '80s, odd pockets of the land were put to flax by an enterprising farmer who thought that the crop would yield a good return, but essentially, large-scale cultivation of flax in Scotland seems to be gone. Which is a pity, not least for the loss of the swaying fields of blue flowers;

there can be few crops which produce such a picturesque addition to the farming year.

The First Statistical Account of 1791 shows that the acreages of flax were largest in the eastern and south-western parts of Scotland. Indeed, in some parishes, for example Lochmaben in Dumfries and Galloway and Kirkden in Angus, women weavers spun all the flax they could grow and imported more. Prior to this period, however, the linen industry had a chequered history, although a boost to manufacture had arrived with the somewhat macabre Act of Parliament of 1686 which insisted that the dead should be buried dressed in Scottish linen.

By 1845, according to the Second Statistical Account, 400,000 tons of flax were imported from the Baltic countries. Throughout Scotland, the amount of flax grown rarely amounted to more than an acre per tenant, and that only supplied the tenant's own domestic needs for clothing the family, and so on. Indeed the same Statistical Account showed that some places had given up growing flax altogether, and generally the crop was grown on a decreasing acreage. Already, in 1795, a minister in Tibbermore in Perthshire was saying that 'Flax is by no means a crop high in the farmers' estimation; besides the trouble attending to it, it adds nothing to the dunghill.'

In fact, there was little reason to keep growing the crop after the ending of the government subsidies in the early nineteenth century. The whole business of growing flax, followed closely by the treatment it then required to end up as linen, was labour-intensive and fraught with problems. Looked at from the comfortable viewpoint of the twentieth century, it is not altogether surprising that this laborious process rapidly fell out of favour.

Flax seed was sown at the end of April, preferably after a shower, when the ground was wet, following a crop of oats, pease, barley or, most often, after potatoes. The fully grown plant was later harvested by hand, being pulled out by the roots in bunches, and tied into small sheaves. Thereafter, a variety of processes was necessary before the fibres were ready for spinning.

First, the seed pods were removed, drawing the flax through a wide, coarse rippling comb. It was drawn gently through iron teeth and then gathered, in small sheaves, into a bundle which would be tied up with a length of flax. These sheaves were then steeped in a retting pond, or lint hole, so that the fibre could be separated from the bark and woody core. Generally, retting was carried out straightaway after rippling, but in the Melrose area some folk kept their flax in sacks and threshed it lightly with a flail in spring to release the seed before retting the remaining stalks.

Retting was best done in stagnant, peaty water, though most places used whatever was available, since an Act passed in the Scottish Parliament in 1606 prohibited the laying of 'ony grene lynt' in lochs and running streams. The reason behind this diktat was that substances released by the soaking flax were detrimental to fish.

After a couple of weeks in the retting pond, the sheaves were removed, spread out in a grassy field and allowed to dry. They were then beaten on a stone block with a mallet or flax mell, to break the core of the fibre. This was followed by scutching, using an instrument like a butcher's cleaver, reportedly a dusty job. Since scutching did not remove all the superfluous material, an instrument resembling a large pair of curling tongs, known as a clove or stripper, could be used. Small bunches of fibre were dragged through iron jaws and all unwanted pieces were scraped off. Part of an old iron barrel was best for making the jaws of the clove, it was said.

The final stage, splitting the fibres, was done by drawing the flax over boards set with rows of metal teeth. This process was called heckling.

If some of these expressions and words sound familiar, it is because a few have survived into the present day. Modern hackles are still made, adapted from use with linen first to jute and now to artificial fibres. Although you won't find hacklemakers listed in a business directory today, travellers crossing the Tay Road Bridge can glance to the east on the Dundee side. There, a wooden structure which housed the team of naval architects responsible for Captain Robert Falcon Scott's ship *Discovery* also housed, until a decade ago, the firm of William R. Stewart & Sons, Hacklemakers.

*

Linen was generally woven by individual weavers, who would have a loom upstairs in the attic of their house or in a shed at the back. As time went on into the nineteenth century, the flax was imported 'raw' and dressed, spun and woven in Scotland, and the industry became larger.

After the dressing came the bleaching, for the finer linens. Many riverside settlements are still marked on maps as 'Bleach-fields', and often a business such as a laundry or dyers replaced the earlier bleach-works. Many of the surviving laundries in Scotland owe their origins to bleaching of linen.

Each small area would have many weavers mentioned in their records. Merchants in Dysart in Fife had at one point 1,000 looms, spread around a ten-mile radius. These weavers would sell their wares to a central dealer, who would generally export the surplus as far afield as London. In the late eighteenth century, several small burghs also appointed their own linen stamp master whose job it was to ensure that the quality of the local product met with government standards for export from the area. Some places became famous for their damask, such as Kirkcaldy and Dunfermline, but most small weavers wove sheeting, ticking and coarse brown linen for everyday use, plus a small surplus for sale.

The advent of machinery and the power loom gradually eroded the viability of the village weavers, but the large manufacturing industries of weaving now prospered until the First World War, especially the flourishing export market to the USA. After the war, the market in the USA was never substantially re-established, and the financial Depression of 1929, both in the USA and at home, as well as a massive upsurge of cheaper imports, effectively killed off most of the Scottish linen industry.

It is well worth studying Ordnance Survey maps to find evidence of 'lint mills', many of which still remain alongside a mill lade.

As late as 1945, when fabric was nearly impossible to find, crafty housewives would buy up more recent architectural drawings, as they had been sketched on waxed linen. By boiling off the wax, the residual linen could be made into clothes.

*

The House of Dun near Montrose is owned and run by the National Trust for Scotland. Ian Dale of Angus Weavers Ltd is one of the Trust's tenants there, and, housed in the old courtyard, he declares himself to be 'one of the sole survivors of the linen weavers'. This is indeed true. In his flourishing business not only does he produce on the magnificent old looms linen tablecloths and traditional huckaback, a coarser linen with raised designs upon its surface, but also vibrant damasks in rich colours, sometimes with metallic silver and gold thread, for the great houses and mansions of the world. His work is a living testament to the highly prized skills once commonplace in Scotland.

Ian Dale's transition into a weaver was long routed, although he first became interested in linen weaving while still a schoolboy in Angus, when the family still owned a handloom. At that time, there were still weavers working in Laurencekirk and Luthermuir and in the 1950s sons of weavers often helped out as a means of earning pocket money. It was on these looms that Ian first learned to wind bobbins, then operate a single pedal Jacquard handloom. After graduating he worked overseas as an engineer in the textile industry, returning to Scotland in 1980 when he bought out the same business where he had first learned to pitch a shuttle as a boy. Today, Angus Weavers Ltd are the sole survivors of a craft that once employed over 80,000 at its height in the 1800s.

The wooden loom frames that Angus Weavers use today date from the end of the eighteenth century. The first cast-iron Jacquard machines made in Lyon were bridged over these wooden frames in the 1820s, and it is this configuration which allows Angus Weavers to weave plain fabrics with the Jacquard machine standing idle, or very ornate designs woven into the fabric by using the Jacquard mechanism.

Angus Weavers have received wide-ranging commissions, recent examples including a design for Paisley University graduation gowns and fabrics used for the restoration of one of Queen Victoria's favourite residences, Osborne House, the Italianate villa on the Isle of Wight designed by Prince Albert. They have furnished a complete set of period fabrics to refurbish the Great Bed of Ware, including the ornate coverlet incorporating a fine gold thread, for the Victoria and Albert

Ian Dale is one of the National Trust for Scotland's tenants at the House of Dun, by Montrose. He declares himself to be 'one of the sole survivors of the linen weavers'. Here he demonstrates one of the pattern cards for ornate Jacquard weaves.

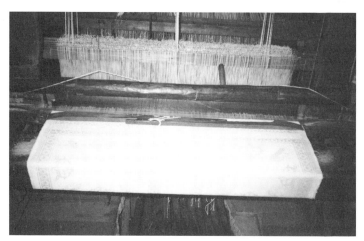

Ian Dale's finished handiwork – linen napkins – produced on old linen weaving looms.

Museum in London, and a set of sixteenth-century Domix hangings for the modern reconstruction of Shakespeare's Globe Theatre, also in London.

But such is the uniqueness of Angus Weavers' operation, commissions have come in from much further afield. In 2002 they completed a commission to design and weave a set of banqueting linens for the governor's mansion house in Virginia incorporating three of the state emblems of Virginia, the American dogwood flower, the Cardinal bird and the crests of the great seal of Virginia.

Much closer to home were drapes for the Great Hall at Muchalls Castle, a seventeenth-century castle originally belonging to the Burnett of Leys family. The castle sits on the picturesque coast between Stonehaven and Aberdeen.

The House of Dun (National Trust for Scotland) is three miles west of Montrose on the A935.

St Cyrus – the bride's measuring stick

The tradition of the bride's bequest at St Cyrus in Aberdeenshire is quite possibly unique, owing its existence to a chance meeting and to the village's former financial dependence on the linen trade.

St Cyrus had suffered a decline with the arrival of spinning machines in Montrose. This had snatched away a staple employment in the parish, that of spinning the yarn for sailcloth. Sailcloth was much in demand in the port and the St Cyrus women appeared to have had a curious method of spinning it. Ignoring the usual use of a wheel, they coiled the flax around their waists and twisted two threads at a time, one in each hand, walking slowly away from a boy turning it at the end of the room.

The arrival of the machine age decimated the finances of the parish, and by 1840 many were destitute and turning to the church for money. Face to face with this poverty came John Orr, the Laird of Bridgeton. He was so moved by the plight of a young couple he met on their way to be married at St Cyrus Kirk that he changed his will, and the St Cyrus dowries came into being. The

Bride Alison Ramage is officially measured by the Revd Wilson, using the St Cyrus measuring stick (Photo courtesy Van Werminick Photographers, Montrose).

interest from Orr's donation of £1,000 was to be divided into five. One-fifth was to be given to needy old folk. The other four-fifths was to be divided into dowries and given to the youngest, oldest, tallest and shortest bride each year. The oldest and youngest were easy for the minister to establish from their birth certificates. But their height? Hence the bride's measuring stick.

Each bride married at St Cyrus is measured for her height (future brides may be reassured this is the only measurement taken!). The measuring is carried out by the minister, using a stick specially provided for the purpose. The bride must also 'undo her hair, so that her tresses may hang loosely over her shoulder and add nothing to her stature'. This custom has continued for more than 150 years, although the infrequency of marriages taking place within the kirk means that the measuring stick has little use today. The conditions of the bequest were probably strictly adhered to in earlier days.

St Cyrus (Aberdeenshire) lies about five miles north of Montrose on the A92.

Beavershire, by Blairgowrie

Although the beaver has been extinct in Scotland for around 500 years, historically the lowly little animal has been surprisingly important to generations of Scots.

Just to the east of modern-day Blairgowrie, on the road leading to Alyth, is a habitation named on old maps as Beavershire. The name was dropped at the end of the nineteenth century. Almost no certainty can be given to the reasoning behind the naming of this unremarkable hamlet – in fact, the name is sometimes found as 'Bevershire' and other spellings. However, the association of Scotland with the beaver and as home to the beaver is well documented.

Some estimates place beavers in Scotland some 10,500 years ago and they are thought to have been fairly widespread. In December 1788, Dr William Farquharson of Invercauld by Braemar donated to the Society of Antiquaries some beaver bones found near Blairgowrie; other remains have been found, for example, in Berwickshire, Lockerbie and Caithness. Details of finds crop up in Morayshire, where Admiral Duff of Drummuir found bones in a small cave in a sandstone quarry on his estate near Hopeman, on the Moray coast. More recently, an excavation at Edinburgh Castle revealed a beaver incisor dating from the early medieval period.

Many sites are put forward as having borne witness to the symbolic killing of the last Scottish wolf, the most likely contender being Inverness-shire, where in 1743 a Mackintosh killed a wolf on the clan's homelands. The fate of the last beaver, however, is far more obscure. Its disappearance is open to wide speculation.

Some historical accounts claim that the Scottish beaver was scarce as early as the twelfth century, others that there were still beavers around in the sixteenth century. Evidence in Europe suggests that beaver meat was available in Holland during the Crusades. The tail and paws were eaten like fish; the glands contained an aspirin-like substance used in medicine; and the skin was highly prized. But it was the sleek, highly attractive and usefully waterproof fur, a covering thought by man to suit himself more than the beaver, which led ultimately to the creature's demise.

While beavers may have been eradicated in Scotland, it was mainly Scots who were to benefit from the beaver trade in Canada. Scots filled almost every available vacancy in the Hudson's Bay Company, as the rugged characters from remote areas of Scotland were ideally suited to the loneliness and extreme conditions of northern Canada's lengthy winters. As late as 1920, my mother recalls a Scot visiting her family home in north Vancouver, sitting contentedly with his husky dog in the sitting room, uttering hardly a word, so used to silence had he become in his working life.

Scots employees operated on a system of nepotism that ensured any cousin, brother or favoured acquaintance was found a position. A recent account of the Hudson's Bay Company lists fifty-two employees whose surnames were prefixed with 'Mac', and this account covers a mere fifty years of the Company's 250 years of beaver trapping, from 1820 to 1870.

Beaver skin hats, coats and slippers were hugely prized in Europe for hundreds of years. In his diaries in the 1660s, Samuel Pepys noted that he had bought a beaver hat for the then massive sum of eighty-five shillings. Furthermore, this treasured item of attire was afforded an honoured place in his wardrobe, being replaced, when it was raining, by a rabbit skin hat, good enough for inclement weather.

Wearing a hat fashioned from beaver skin was a statement of one's superior station in life. So desirable were beaver hats that in France generous trade-ins were given for worn models when making a new purchase. These secondhand hats were then sent off to Spain, where, stripped of the badly worn parts, they were swapped, incredibly, for African ivory.

In France, hats had traditionally been made from woollen felt, but in 1323 a government order gave permission to the grander Parisian 'chaperonniers', who used mainly the superior lambswool, to switch over and produce hats from the much finer material of beaver skin.

Beaver, especially the fine underside of the animal, gave the lustrous appearance denied to wool, and possessed the enviable advantages, in the days before umbrellas, of being both waterproof and lightweight. Beaver fur was not only beautiful and practical but also fashionable, rare and expensive. Demand increased, unfortunately for the poor beavers, which were hunted down in their hundreds of thousands.

A huge source of beaver existed as yet unknown, well beyond the Atlantic horizons. Meanwhile the European beaver was captured, skinned and exported to Paris and London. Geoffrey Chaucer's rich merchant sported a beaver hat on his Canterbury pilgrimage in the late fourteenth century, while the trousseau of Blanche de Bourbon, ill-fated bride of Pedro of Castile in 1352, included a hat of scarlet velvet and beaver embroidered with gold, pearls and precious stones.

While living, fur is growing and being constantly groomed. It is the construction of each single hair which gives beaver fur its desirability. Each hair, although this is not visible to the naked eye, is notched, and when the longer, outer hairs are removed, the downy underside is then felted. The preparation of beaver fur involved lengthy pounding, steaming, stretching and, by the end of the eighteenth century, the use of mercury and nitric acid, a potent and dangerous cocktail. 'Mad' hatters were commonplace, and not only in *Alice in Wonderland*, as the mercury fumes gave rise to 'hatter's shakes'. The term 'mad hatter' became an accurate description of yet another class to suffer from the demands of fashion.

The beaver hat became an essential accessory for both men and women, shaped into the most fashionable mode of the time. The crowns of hats rose in height, brims became wider. The hats worn by British Beefeaters were made from beaver skin, and remained so for a couple of hundred years. This increase in the size of hat was good news for all involved in the beaver fur trade, the Hudson's Bay Company in particular, most of whose Scots employees dreamed of returning to the shores of Scotland with a fortune in their pocket and a Scots wife with whom to settle down. Few achieved their wish.

Fashions in beaver skin hats in the early seventeenth century had become more and more elaborate. The Scottish crowned head of James I of England and VI of Scotland was only too happy to embrace this fashion, although by now it is almost certain that the beavers who supplied his headgear were long gone from his northern kingdom. He sauntered into London from his home north of the border where he had lived, if not in penury, at least within a very restricted budget. Arriving in the wake of the extravagance and ostentation of the late Elizabethan court, he rose to new heights of spending and fashion, and this included millinery extravaganzas.

James ordered twenty beaver hats, seventeen of them to be black, lined with taffeta, trimmed with black bands and feathers, perhaps for the period of court mourning; there was a black riding hat, embroidered in gold and silver trimmed with a flat plume. His wife, Anne of Denmark, was very fashion-conscious, and their son also sported feather-strewn hats ordered by his father.

This was a considerable extravagance. Beaver cost about twenty times more than the equivalent hat made of woollen felt, and up-and-coming tradesmen in William Fennor's *The Counter's Commonwealth* (1616) were advised: 'Your four shilling Dutch felt hat shall be converted to a three pound beaver.' The European, purely commercial chase for the beaver replaced the traditional respect shown to the animal by the Native Americans. A Montagnais chief listed the beaver's attributes in wonder: 'The beaver does everything perfectly well. He makes us kettles, axes, swords, knives and gives us drink and food without the trouble of cultivating the ground ... .'

The same attitude was seen with the bison a century or so later, when the majestic animal, just before being hunted almost to extinction, was seen by the Native Americans as a walking emporium, supplying hides for shelter, bone for needles and implements, meat for food and so on. At least the beaver appeared to give the hunters more trouble for their money.

After remaining desirable for more than 200 years, a change in the wind of fashion gave the beaver a breather. Prince Albert appeared at the opening of the Great Exhibition in 1851 wearing a silk hat. In a tilting of the royal headgear, he demonstrated that the previously impossible task of constructing a silk covered hat on a muslin base was solved and the beaver was never again to be so much in demand.

There have been attempts at re-introducing the beaver in the past. The Marquis of Bute tried to settle Canadian beavers, which are larger than the European type, near to Rothesay on the Isle of Bute, a population which increased but then died out by 1890. Reports also tell vaguely of an attempt at Brodie, near Nairn. If beavers are eventually successfully re-introduced to Scotland, they will at least be able to live in peace, safe in the knowledge that their days as a fashion statement are over.

Beavershire no longer exists on maps. The original place was around three miles east of Blairgowrie, on the A926.

Embroidery village

The womenfolk of Houston village in Renfrewshire supported an embroidery business which lasted, rather like their counterparts in Paisley shawl weaving, for almost exactly 100 years. One of their most famous commissions was the rich embroidered curtain which hung behind Queen Victoria's dais at the 1851 Great Exhibition. The success of this work then led to a commission for embroidering the chair cushions for the new House of Lords at Westminster. These were embroidered on Utrecht velvet. They disappeared many years ago when the seats were re-covered in hide.

The Paisley weavers created ever more intricate and beautiful shawls for a full century and suffered their demise because of the vagaries of fashion. Their famous shawls, which changed shape to suit the changing shape of skirts, were ideal for use with a crinoline, over which a conventional coat would not do. Mass-market cheaper versions were developed, becoming so popular that almost every woman could afford to own one, and with that, the advent of the bustle and the demise of the crinoline, the Paisley shawl finally fell out of fashion.

Houston embroidery lasted until it was eventually overtaken by machine work. It was greatly influenced by the arrival of one young man, Matthew King, who arrived in Houston in 1820, aged seventeen, with the express intention of learning weaving and then returning to Glasgow to set himself up in business.

Houston was then a thriving village with a growing population. The population in 1801 was recorded as 1,891, and by 1841 had risen to 2,818. The Statistical Account of 1791 explains that the village then had forty-two looms engaged in the principal trade of weaving cottons, muslins, lawn and silk gauze. These skills clearly produced a healthy economy within the village and 'many of the young women and girls in the village made flower muslin, by which they not only maintain themselves but buy fineries – the congregation on the Sabbath appears like an assembly of well dressed and fashionable women' (most of the embroidery done by the Houston women was the traditional Ayrshire work, that of white on white or 'flowering').

Matthew King never returned to Glasgow to set up his business. Instead, in 1825 he married an embroiderer, Jean Barr of Houston, and made his home there. Little seems to be known about King's background, but he turned out to be an enterprising businessman. He set up his headquarters at home and employed embroiderers from Bridge of Weir, Kilbarchan, Lochwinnoch, Beith, Kilmacolm, Port Glasgow, Paisley, Greenock, Johnstone, Inchinnan, Bishopton and Stevenston.

King had established a business link with Messrs Houldsworth of Manchester and they seemed impressed enough with the Houston work to send embroidery work there instead of to Paisley as formerly. At this time a Mr Fulton of Paisley brought back from the Continent a gauze dress which had been embroidered with coloured threads at a French convent. King organised six of his embroiderers to copy it.

In King's time the embroiderers could see the coloured originals at first hand. Many samples of foreign work were used as ideas or prototypes for the Houston work. King's daughter Jean, even as a young girl, was particularly gifted at puzzling out new stitches, and it was said that when she was out playing her father often called her in to work out the stitches used in some sample from abroad. Many of her copies were of a finer finish than the originals.

THE LADY ANNE SPEIRS'

CLASS FOR

HOUSTON EMBROIDERY

Meets on WEDNESDAYS, at VILLAGE HALL,

AT EIGHT P.M.

Teachers.

MISS KING.	MISS J. KING.
MISS MAGGIE WHYTEHILL.	MISS AGNES M. EWING.

Secretary and Treasurer.

MR. GEORGE YOUNG.

Entry=Money Collectors, MRS. G. YOUNG AND LADY ANNE SPEIRS.

FOR MATERIALS APPLY TO Miss AGNES M'KAY.

Charge, 1/6 for 6 Lessons. To be paid in advance.

Out of this there are the expenses and rent of Village Hall, and some of the Teachers' expenses to be defrayed.

Materials are sold at the Class at the lowest price. But, if considered too expensive or too good quality, could be got elsewhere.

Small gifts and donations to the Class, besides the kind way in which so many have given their services gratuitously, has enabled our Treasurer to increase the number of lessons to 6 from 4 for the 1/6 entry-money.

ANNE SPEIRS.

In order to encourage young women to come forward and learn embroidery for the Houston embroidery trade, advertisements such as these were commonly seen in the Houston area.

This surviving wooden block used by the Houston embroiderers still has
evidence of the blue dye used to transfer the pattern onto fabric.

A large number of the wooden blocks used to print the patterns
on the fabric have survived and can be seen at the Paisley Museum
upon advance request, along with two napkins dating from 1888
and two large bedcovers from 1887. Glasgow Museums have
other items in their collection.

Matthew King seems to have been very much respected by all
who knew him, and this indicated his status as a good employer.
Apparently he paid his workers from his own money, rather than
deprive them if customers held money back for discount purposes.
However, the business came under threat. On 1 January 1867 the
only son of Matthew and Jean King died relatively young. The
shock and grief which his father suffered caused him to partially
lose his sight, and he himself died in 1875. (The entire family is
buried in Houston churchyard with a full memorial stone.)

The demand for embroidery was also threatened by the arrival
of machines, which produced work cheaper and faster. Hand-
embroidery industries were failing all over the country, for
example in Mauchline, where the trade ceased abruptly and
entirely, causing great suffering. However, the fortunes of the

Houston embroiderers received a fillip and small revival later in the century.

In the meantime, on Matthew King's death his daughters, Jean and Ann, carried on the business. Before the young Mr King died, he had encouraged his sisters to undertake private orders at the request of Mrs Speirs of Elderslie. Her printing block has the initials GSE and was made specially to mark her orders. This saved the trade for some time. The first private order stamped and prepared by Jeannie King and worked by the Houston embroiderers was a dress for Mrs Spiers, which she wore at Court. It was by all accounts much admired. The exact date is unknown, but it must have been in the 1860s or early 1870s.

An article in the *Glasgow Herald* of 8 May 1888 contained a report on an exhibition of Houston work currently being produced. The occasion seems to have been shortly after the coming-of-age of the young laird, Mr A Speirs. He offered to give prizes for the samples of embroidery being worked by women still under instruction. Miss Ann Ring, although hindered by deafness, taught an embroidery class. Lady Anne Speirs produced many of the designs and in addition to some of the work being for sale, prizes were awarded on the recommendation of a London judge.

The *Glasgow Herald* report commented on the brash colours used in the Houston work, and suggested that artistically coloured patterns instead of simple coloured outlines might help the embroiderers to work in a better blend of colours. Few of the embroiderers by this time would be likely to see the original examples of coloured embroideries from abroad, and so would have little idea of the colour schemes then fashionable.

This exhibition and the giving of prizes did evince a revival, and many of the daughters and grand-daughters of the old Houston workers were keen to join the staff involved in the revival. However, by the beginning of the twentieth century the industry had finally lost so much trade that it was unable to survive.

Houston, Renfrewshire, is on the junction of the B789 and the B790 a couple of miles east of Bridge of Weir. Paisley Museum is on the High Street in Paisley.

The Girls' Friendly Society

In the Paisley Hostel Hall of the Girls' Friendly Society there was is a blackboard which still outlines the instructions given in English for the benefit of Gaelic-speaking girls from the north-west of Scotland and the outer isles. The girls were in Glasgow for the simple purpose of earning a living, and this being the late nineteenth century, the first and only language of most of these young arrivals was the Gaelic. They came over to earn a living either in domestic service or, in large number, by employment within the Coates thread-mills.

The girls were there under the protection and with the good offices of the Girls' Friendly Society, an organisation founded in 1875. Soon the Scottish Girls' Friendly Society spread throughout the length and breadth of Scotland, its girls guided and watched over by dedicated ladies who took life and their role in the new society with whole-hearted seriousness. The society mainly aimed at providing accommodation and moral guidance for girls who were far from home and 'in service'. It provided hostels, holiday homes and (where necessary) training, but paramount in all this was the moral welfare of their charges. Indeed the ladies in charge bound themselves to a strict code of conduct.

The rules of the society in its infancy stipulated that 'No girl shall be admitted to membership without a period of definite preparation ... the length of this period will vary according to circumstances, but should not be for less than three months.' The ladies had to be single when they joined, but were allowed to continue membership when they married if they busied themselves with fundraising and held to the rules of the society. Members were expected to:

- avoid reading bad books and magazines
- endeavour to spread no scandal and to repeat no idle tale of the disadvantage of others
- avoid all exaggerated fashions and dress simply
- pray morning and evening
- attend the meetings on Thursdays
- read a portion of the Bible at least once a day.

The society flourished and a sick fund was established, circulating libraries were formed and older members were given financial assistance when in need. It was indeed a friendly society in all the best traditions of those societies, while keeping an eagle eye on the young girls in its hostels. Before the Second World War, no hostel girl was allowed to talk to a stranger. This would have been difficult enough at the best of times, as they were not allowed out for walks on their own: they had to go in 'crocodile formation'!

Gradually the need for such an organisation waned, and the society finally closed in 1990, distributing the considerable sums gathered over the years and from the sale of property to other Scottish charities.

Mother Buchan

In the late 1790s the two-handed spinning-wheel was successfully introduced into Galloway, and was used with unrivalled skill by a collection of ladies at Larghill, close to Crocketford. The village lies almost midway between Dumfries and Castle Douglas, in Dumfries and Galloway region.

Weaving wool was a means of support upon which the community's economic survival depended. They belonged to one of the strangest of religious sects in Scottish history and were ostracised from nearly every area in which their group attempted to settle. Their official name was the 'Buchanites', and their leader's name 'Mother Buchan'.

Mother Buchan was born plain Elspeth Simpson in the parish of Fordyce, Banffshire. On the death of her mother she was brought up by a relative, who appeared to give her a good basic education. This relative then married a West Indian planter. Elspeth was to take passage with her from Greenock, when, according to the story, she took a distinct fancy to the 'gay life of the town' and jumped ship before it sailed. She worked in domestic service, eventually marrying one of her master's workers, a potter called Robert Buchan, who quickly realised he had taken on a flighty and headstrong wife. Reasoning that she would settle down better back home in Banff, he moved the family there, but his pottery failed, and he ran off to Glasgow, leaving Elspeth and their children to their fate.

Elspeth was nothing if not innovative. She promptly opened a Dame school, but developed at the same time a religious fanaticism, fasting for weeks and ignoring her children, eventually incurring the wrath of her neighbours, who drove her out of town and back into the exasperated arms of her husband in Glasgow.

Her fervour for religion of any persuasion was undiminished, and after hearing a sermon preached by the Revd Hugh White of Irvine, she wrote to him, effected a meeting, and influenced him to such an extent with her unorthodox views (of which more later) that the established church charged him with heresy. This charge he ignored and was promptly ejected from the church.

The two of them now lived in Irvine, and such was the fervour and extremity of Buchan's preaching that the group's meetings had to be held after dark to avoid disruption. The fear and distaste Elspeth Buchan engendered was simple to understand, for she had by now declared herself to be the woman described in Revelation 12: 'There appeared a great wonder in Heaven: a woman clothed with the sun, and the moon under her feet, and upon her head a crown of twelve stars.'

The life of the group fell into a distinct pattern. They would settle briefly in a community, cause uproar with their views and be hounded out, and either Mother Buchan was hauled back to be dumped with her husband, or they by chance happened upon some welcoming convert who offered them sanctuary in another part of Scotland. So the tale of Mother Buchan, Hugh White and their small band of followers is one of criss-crossing the country one step ahead of an angry mob.

Their departure from a temporary refuge in Muthill, Perthshire, was typically rapid. The gang 'voluntarily quitted the place likewise, and with such precipitation that some of them never shut the door behind them; one left a washing on the green, another a cow bellowing at the crib without food or anyone to mind her.' But Mother Buchan herself fled in style. A cart was found to speed her on her way (as she was unused to tramping, a surprising fact in view of her incessant travelling to date) and, flamboyantly dressed in a scarlet robe, she led her little following of forty or fifty folk. According to a contemporary account they consisted of 'clever chiels and bonnie, spanking rosy-cheeked lassies, many of them in their teens'.

Down to the south-west they trailed, settling for a while at New Cample Farm, a mile south of Thornhill, by Dumfries, until once more attacked by the locals, who took exception to White describing Mother Buchan as

> the mysterious woman predicted in Revelation, in whom the light of God was restored to the world, where it had not been since the ascension of Christ, but where it would now continue till the period of translation into the clouds to meet the Lord at his second coming.

By now the rules of the community were established. Marriage was abolished and the children became the property of the community. They worked for neighbouring farmers, but never accepted payment. How they managed without any obvious income is unknown; possibly each new convert gave enough of his or her worldly goods to ensure the group's survival.

But no rampaging neighbours or disappointments could dim the fervour of the group and their leader. During their sojourn at New Cample Farm, they rode out two false alarms of their ascent into Heaven. The first time, Mother Buchan suddenly took the heat out of the occasion by informing her followers that unfortunately she had decided they were not yet quite prepared to rise up and she would smoke her pipe instead. On the second occasion, she started preparations further in advance and ordered forty days fasting for everyone except herself and White, an announcement which spurred the local authorities into action, fearing infanticide. But they found nothing incriminating and on the appointed hour the weakened followers, their heads shorn of all but a top-knot (so that God would find it easier to pluck them up to Heaven), dragged themselves to the nearby Templand Hill, where they were to watch Mother Buchan in full splendour stand on a wooden stage and call upon the Almighty. However, instead of the followers ascending (their additional preparations had included wearing light bauchels or slippers, easily kicked off when the moment came) Mother Buchan suffered a swift descent. The wind gusted, her platform toppled and she crashed to the ground.

As the group straggled back to the farm, she was quick to blame others for this fiasco. No doubt in a better state of health than those who had fasted for forty days, she was quick-witted enough to blame their lack of faith for this non-event.

But it was all too much for most of the followers, many of whom now deserted the group, while the Kirk Session of Closeburn, increasingly alarmed by events, summoned White to give assurances that no member of the group would be a burden on the parish. White was unable to do this, so the remainder of the following managed to procure the farm of Auchengibbert, between Dumfries and Castle Douglas.

Here they spun and wove, dyeing their clothes the distinctive pale green which both sexes wore. The movement now seemed to be less eccentric, and ceased to attract converts. White especially tried to mask the excesses of the movement, which led almost to a split between him and Buchan. But although she was a sick woman, she defied the imminence of death almost to the last. She died on 29 March 1791, having decreed that she was merely off to paradise to arrange for their coming and citing various possibilities about her eventual re-appearance, all dependent on the faith of her followers of course. If they were faithful, she would come back after six days, and they would all rise up to Heaven together. If not this period would be extended to ten years, or fifty. It depended on their faith.

After her death, the dissension between White and the others came to a head. White wanted to have her buried, the others wanted her body to be hidden in the farmhouse. The Sheriff enquired into the burial of the body and was successfully fooled by the group into believing that a burial had taken place in Kirkgunzeon churchyard. In fact, the body had been packed away in 'dry feathers and deposited under the kitchen hearth'.

And so things might have stayed, but the story was not quite ended yet. White made a break with the movement and sailed with thirty followers to Newcastle, Delaware, where their fate is unknown. The remnant struggled on, waiting with bated breath, trying to overcome successive disappointments as the anniversaries of Buchan's death passed without her re-appearance.

They finally moved to Crocketford, building houses to the cost of £1,000 and living in Newhouse, to which dwelling the dwindling flock of twelve followers carted the body of Mother Buchan.

The last of the Buchanites, Andrew Innes and his wife, eagerly awaited the fiftieth anniversary of her death, which passed uneventfully, a disappointment from which Andrew never quite recovered. His wife died at the end of November 1845, and when he felt his own death was drawing near he admitted to friends that Mother Buchan's body was still in the house. When he died, he asked that her body be placed with his, but underneath, so that when she arose, she would have to wake him up first.

Apparently this was done, and the story goes that the pair of them were buried in a small enclosure behind the house. No one appears to have taken a further interest in this story, least of all digging up the ground to discover what, if anything, lurks beneath.

Crocketford, Dumfries and Galloway, is on the A75 midway between Castle Douglas and Dumfries.

2

Animals, stones and superstitions

The whalebone arch

Times and attitudes have changed massively since, in 1922, a huge whale ended its life in the Western Isles, an area it would have been wise to avoid as the whaling industry was in full spate. No thought was given at that time to the possible extinction of these magnificent creatures, nor indeed to methods of hunting and killing them. So when a blue whale came ashore at the village of Bragar on the west coast of Lewis in 1922, it was recorded as the largest whale ever in the northern hemisphere and there was general and popular interest.

There was a whaling station on Harris for a number of years and one of their catchers had harpooned this massive creature but it escaped to die a long and slow death. The stun explosive charge in the nose cone of the harpoon had not exploded. The harpoon goes in as a pencil shape and the three barbs are supposed to expand outwards to prevent removal. This happened, but not in the expected sequence, and the failure of the stun charge allowed the whale to dive deep taking with it many hundreds of feet of rope. Whether the rope snapped or the catcher cut it to prevent the boat going down is not known.

The whale drifted onto some rocks at the entrance to a small cave and there it became wedged. The locals extracted quite a lot of blubber from it but that had limited use. After some time the whole carcase began to give off an odour that with an onshore wind was proving unpleasant.

Murdo Morrison's father, also a Murdo, was the local postmaster and shopkeeper at Bragar. He decided that a whalebone arch over the back gateway to the house would be appropriate and to this end he removed – or got others to remove – the lower jaw. This was taken out on horse-drawn sledges in two sections.

Local school children gathered underneath the Whalebone Arch in the village of Bragar on the west coast of Lewis in 1922. This popular postcard was entitled 'One hundred little Jonahs'.

After some months pillars were built, the whole structure erected and the harpoon affixed. It was during this process that the enterprise nearly came to an abrupt and violent end. The blacksmith who was working on the harpoon discovered to his surprise, and the surprise of some onlookers as well, that the explosive charge had never exploded. It proceeded to do so, and buried itself in the end of the shop, almost cancelling out a long line of Morrison descendants.

The whalebone has featured in thousands of photographs down through the years. In recent times it began to show wear and tear necessitating renovation. This has now been carried out and it is back in its original location, ready for a few hundred more years.

At one time there was a photograph, made into a postcard, that showed a large group of local school children gathered on staging underneath the whalebone with the caption 'One hundred little Jonahs'. More recently there was a proposal that, as a millennium project, the whalebone should be re-sited on a nearby hillock and covered in copper to make it look like a gigantic fish spine, but the answer from the locals was an overwhelming 'No'.

It has survived in its current position for nearly a century, and this despite being the subject of many offers and even a threat from the Kirk. One of the many proposals was an offer of purchase from Lord Leverhulme in the 1920s, when he was resident on the island. He wanted it for the entrance to his castle and offered £1,000 for it. To his credit, Murdo Morrison the postmaster refused, despite the dangling of such a large sum and the undoubted temptation of such an easy way to gain a windfall.

There was also a snort of disapproval from the more strident members of the Kirk who reckoned it was a dangerous attraction for folk on the Sabbath, this being an island where the children's swings in the play park were tied up on Sundays to prevent their use. But finally, even Hitler did not disturb the archway, although there was a passing thought locally that it provided a landmark for enemy aircraft. The arch remained standing and, now renovated, there is stays, more than eighty years after its arrival on the shores of Lewis.

Bragar, on the island of Lewis, is along the A858 on the north-west coast of the island, about fourteen miles from Stornoway.

Pig trough or font?

The dual carriageway up the slight incline to South Dalziel Parish Church frames the church with a dreary, anonymous view of the modern town of Motherwell. Sandwiched between a police station and an industrial estate at the rear, the church itself looks stranded in the twenty-first century. But the lofty, impeccably kept church interior reveals a silent indifference to the traffic outside.

The present church was constructed in 1789, with scant regard to the comfort of the congregation, who attended less frequently in winter owing to the lack of proper flooring. The worshippers sat with their feet on the cold, damp clay and the Revd James Clason, minister from 1786 to 1801, declared that the church was 'one of the coldest in Scotland'. Nevertheless the church thrived and in 1860 the building was extended – and floored – to accommodate the larger congregation.

Little now remains of the original Dalziel medieval parish church, as it now lies under the nearby Mausoleum of the Hamiltons of Dalziel, but the font, a relic of the ancient church, now sits in a prominent position within the 'new' church.

The twelfth-century stone font, now back in use at South Dalziel Church in Motherwell was originally within a pre-Reformation church which stood on a site nearby. When the church was demolished after 1560, the font was used as a pig trough until the nineteenth century, when the Duke of Hamilton rescued it.

The font now being used in South Dalziel Parish Church has been put to many unexpected uses. Cleaned and restored, it shows few signs of its age, which dates back to at least the twelfth century. Not that it has been in constant use as a font. Its most notable use was as a pig trough and it probably spent a few years tossed to one side in the undergrowth somewhere; in fact, the most remarkable fact about the font is that it is in use today, having been the subject of a remarkable rescue.

After the Reformation in 1560, St Patrick's (the medieval church) had a change of name and was then called the Church of Dalziel. Eventually, the church fell into such a state of disrepair that it was decided to demolish it and build a new church in a better location. At some point during this demolition, the font was cast out and was in use on the Dalziel estate as a pig trough.

A nineteenth-century Lord Hamilton's attention was attracted by this relic on his estate, and he had the stonework cleaned and presented the font to the South Dalziel Parish Church where it continues to be used for its original purpose today.

Motherwell is about twelve miles south-east of Glasgow, just off the M74 southbound at Junction 6. After leaving the motorway and crossing the bridge, take the first road to the right at the traffic lights, and follow this road all the way to a T-junction. Just ahead is the church, but it is not possible to park a car in front of it. In order to park, take the road to the right and then left and retrace steps to the front door.

The White Horse of Mormond

On the south-western slope of the Mormond Hill stands the proud figure of a white horse. It rises to a height of 126 feet and the body is about 106 feet in breadth. Cut out of the turf, the outline is filled with the white quartz indigenous to the hill. Its construction must have been a considerable feat; it achieves a remarkable artistic success, and the cost must have only been possible with the aid of a wealthy patron.

When and why such a huge landmark came to be in that place is not certain, but one theory is that it arrived on the hillside in about 1773 through the efforts of a Captain Fraser, a somewhat

No one is quite sure of the exact date when this White Horse was carved out of the hillside and filled with local white quartz. Only once in its *c*.250-year history has it been filled in – during the Second World War, when it was felt it might attract enemy fire.

eccentric son of Lord Strichen, a judge of the Court of Session. Several other theories have been put forward as to its origins. One was simply that it imitated the White Horse on the Wiltshire Downs. Another was that the horse commemorated the return of a laird whose horse was slain in war, the landmark being erected by the tenantry. Yet another theory was that it recorded the laird driving a carriage and pair over the hill.

None of these theories is ever likely to be established as the truth now, but the horse stands proud to this day. Only briefly did it vanish from view, during the Second World War, when its whiteness, thought to be a rather obvious marker for the enemy, was camouflaged.

On the crest of the hill also stands Hunters Lodge. The reason for the existence of this building is also unclear, and it bears the abstruse inscription 'In this Hunters Lodge Roy Gibb commands MDCCCLXXIX'.

In *The Howes of Buchan* written by William Anderson in 1865 there are reports of the Lodge harbouring a ghost:

Whether it be Roy's ghost which gets the credit for the present habitation, we know not; but there is a rather well-authenticated story extant of a clever fellow of a keeper, who so traded upon the evil reputation of the place as to induce the laird to raise his salary once or twice. But the appeals for increase became so frequent that the laird resolved to entrap the wary spirit, which came to grief by chance upon the discovery that the keeper's wife produced the 'erf' sounds identified with the visits of the ghost by a cord with a piece of wood in an empty barrel!

The White Horse can be seen on the Mormond Hill from the village of Strichen, Aberdeenshire. Strichen is about fourteen miles from Peterhead on the A950, A952 and then the B9093.

Horse ferry

The innkeeper at Inver in the early twentieth century was the owner of a very docile and obedient horse which, for a modest charge, had the task of transporting hill-walkers and early tourists across the River Feardar, just west of where it merges with the River Dee. The horse, having dropped off his customer at the other side of the river, obediently turned around and came straight back, ready for the next customer. The task may sound as though it was gentle and straightforward, but the river, normally shallow and little wider than a single-track road at this point, was not always easily crossed.

The *Deeside Field* magazine of 1935 reported an eyewitness account of a spectacular cloudburst which occurred on Wednesday 13 July 1927, after a bridge had been built. The Feardar burn became a torrent, and showed signs of engulfing the bridge. Hesitating about crossing the bridge was a sixteen-horse-power Wolseley with five ladies (the writer coyly described them as being no longer in the first flush of youth) from Lanark on board. The chauffeur of the car was advised by onlookers to 'rush it', which he unwisely attempted to do. The car was swept up by the swelling water and whizzed round a few times before fortunately

The Inver Hotel boasted a ferry with a difference – a horse which, having transported its passengers safely over the River Feardar, turned around and came back of its own accord.

coming to rest on the river bank, where the onlookers were able to help the passengers and chauffeur to safety.

These and other stranded motorists at the inn were told by the locals that had the king been in residence he would have opened up the route over the old Brig of Dee at Invercauld and allowed the motorists to travel through the grounds of Balmoral. Within a day the factor at Balmoral, hearing of the plight of the passengers, opened the road of his own accord and the passengers were afforded a special trip through the grounds of Balmoral Estate.

The Inver Inn is on the A93 about three miles west of Crathie and six miles east of Braemar.

'Mareswine'

The *Account of the Shire of Forfar circa 1682* by John Ochterlony Esquire of Guynd is a logical and precise documentation of the area at the time. Reprinted in a limited edition by the Forfar and

District Historical Society in 1969, it is a fascinating insight into life in the area. In general, birds and animals appear to be similar to those seen today, but there were some more unusual animals, described as:

> amphibious creatures bred in the rocks betwixt Arbroath and Ethie [seven miles up the coast from Arbroath], called sea calves; who gender as other beasts doe; and bring forth their young ones in the dry caves and suck them till they be of some bignesse and strength to swim in the water. The old ones are of a huge bignes, nigh to ane ordinare ox, but longer, have no leggs, but in place thereof four finnes, in shape much lyk to a man's hand, whereupon they goe but slowly. In the end September, which is the time they go a land for calving, several in the town of Aberbrothock goe to the caves with boates, and with lighted candles search the caves, where apprehending, they kill diverse of them, both young and old whereof they make very good oyll.

In all probability these were seals, and there is little to suspect about this account, but then the writer goes on to describe something even stranger:

> There is lykwayses ane other creature in shape lyk to ane fish called mareswine, and will be of twenty or four and twenty feet [ten metres] long, all alonst the coast, but especially in the river of Tay, where they are in great abundance, killing a great deal of salmond and doing a great deall of injurie to the fishings. In thir few years there were great numbers cast up dead all alongst the river of Tay, with great wounds and bylings upon ther bodyes, which gave occasion to conjecture that there had been some fight amonst them at sea.

No further details does John Ochterlony divulge, and so this tantalising glimpse of 'mareswine' vanishes back into the mists of the seventeenth century.

Arbroath, Angus, is on the A92 about seventeen miles north-east from Dundee and sixteen miles east from Forfar. Ethie is on the coast about seven miles north of Arbroath.

Earth hounds

'Yird pigs' or 'earth huns' may be confined to Banffshire. I do not know if they have spread further afield, but they sound unpleasant enough for me to earnestly hope that their habitat is totally confined to the Keith area.

In a book published in 1881, *Notes on the Folk-lore of North-east Scotland*, by Walter Gregor, the author vividly describes a 'mysterious dreaded sort of animal, called the "yird swine" ... and believed to live in graveyards, burrowing among the dead bodies and devouring them'. They are reputed to be like a cross between a rat and a rabbit and unique to this area of Scotland.

Local legend has it that these fearful animals abide in Walla kirkyard. The kirkyard sits in a remote position, and, although still in use today, certainly projects an image of other-worldliness and mystery. The oldest graves date from the late eighteenth century. There is a steep drop on a track down to the graveyard, presenting problems in the winter as the track looks as though it could be difficult to traverse in icy conditions. The kirkyard is well away from the church, and the River Deveron rushes close by.

The scamperings of the yird pigs were, mercifully, absent when I visited in full daylight, and it is easy to mock the story as a long-dead myth. But presumably, even if they are not popping out of their burrows every five minutes to be identified by passers-by, the creatures are still very much alive in the imaginations of believers.

What is known is that the church was dedicated to and named after St Walloch, or Volocus, said to have been among the last of the missionaries to be sent to the north-east from St Ninian's centre at Whithorn, and the ancient parish was named Dunmeith. There were at one time two wells, possible remains of which can still be found in the churchyard. These were meant to cure eye infections, and there is note of a child being dipped in the well in 1812. It was the custom of the believer to leave behind a shirt or rag from the child as an offering.

Walla kirkyard sits south of the A920 Dufftown to Huntly road. Leaving Dufftown, proceed about eight miles until a turning south to the right on a secondary road to Haugh of Glass. Immediately after this village, take a road

east to the left and then the first road on the right, going south. Walla Kirk is
about a mile along this road.

Bloodletting altar

The attractive small church of Dunino, Fife, stands across a
magnificent bridge which spans the rushing Dunino burn. The
name Dunino supposedly comes from the Gaelic *Dun Eynach*, or
Dun Nigheana meaning 'fort of the daughters' or 'fort of the broad
moor'. There was a stone circle here, fragments of which were
built into the church. It was almost certainly connected with the
priory of St Andrews around 1253, and it is possible that the
nunnery was in existence before that, although no records remain.
There is a 1698 sundial in the meticulously maintained
churchyard. The stone upon which the sundial stands is believed
to have been carved around AD 800, which makes it one of the
oldest stones in Scottish Christianity. Nearby is a pretty manse.
The church itself appears to thrive and is a place of calm and
beauty.

However, all is not quite as it appears, for within quite literally
a two-minute walk there is a sinister reminder of a much earlier,
much bloodier paganistic past. Park near the church entrance and
immediately in front of you is a grassy track which leads down by
the side of the graveyard wall, in between this and a field. As you
progress downhill and come to the woods and hear the burn you
will be able to follow a clearly marked path. Very soon you come
to a promontory which stands on top of a cliff, below which is the
rushing Dunino burn. On top of this promontory is a round stone
containing, for most of the year, two pools of water. It is said that
this is where the Druidical priest placed his feet before killing his
human sacrificial victim, the blood being caught in the stones and
the body then flung into the burn below.

The hamlet of Dunino, Fife, is about five miles south of St Andrews on the
B9131. The church is to be found by turning east onto a small road, just south
of the school, which is on the west side of the road.

Deathwatch tower

The Dalkeith Watchtower was built in 1827 of red sandstone, and it has a battlement top with narrow arrow-slits on all sides. The tower was built with an upper floor, reached by means of a ladder and trapdoor. An armed watchman stood there all night, his brief being to prevent the digging up of bodies for sale for medical dissection. The tower had been built by a voluntary body called the Committee of the Dalkeith Churchyard Association, sometimes referred to as the Committee for the Protection of the New Burying Ground. The Committee soon discovered, though, that they needed to watch over the watchman, who was himself suspected of neglecting his duties and even of being in collusion

The Dalkeith Watchtower was built in 1827 not to protect the good citizens of the burgh, but to house armed watchmen who kept a sharp look-out for body-snatchers determined to dig up the recently deceased for selling to medical schools for dissection.

with the body-snatchers – a clear case of gamekeeper turned poacher, it would seem.

The Committee and the Kirk Session were soon at odds over who should hold the keys and gain entry in order to spy upon the watchman. The Committee feared that the loss of their sole right of control would weaken the vigilance over the watchmen and lead to the perpetration of the very crime which it was the primary object of the Association to prevent. They warned that the attitude of the Kirk Session would give rise to 'a repetition of the shocking violations which so frequently harrowed up the petitioners [i.e. the Committee] previously to the adoption of the effective system of vigilance'. The Kirk Session in 1829 adopted a resolution rejecting the claims of the Committee and insisting that the keys of the private gate of the burying ground be vested in the hands of some member of the Session. The gate in question was probably located at the North Wynd side of the burial ground where a blocked entrance can still be seen.

Hysteria over the body-snatchers and their crimes reached a peak in the 1820s, and protecting graveyards produced both tragedy and humour. A young man was shot dead in Liberton when he was mistaken for a body-snatcher, when in fact he had merely entered the churchyard for a chat with a friend, and watchers at Fala in Midlothian fired on what they thought to be body-snatchers but which turned out to be the minister's goat.

Dalkeith, Midlothian, is about seven miles south-east of Edinburgh on the A68.

The Clootie Well

A 'clootie well' is a well to which people make a pilgrimage, leaving behind a piece of rag, or 'clootie'. There are several of these wells in the north-east of Scotland. One of the best-known is just outside Munlochy, on the Black Isle. It is easy to recognise, as the passing visitor will suddenly come upon a roadside patch of bushes and trees festooned with rags in various stages of decay, looking as though a rubbish van has accidentally shed its load.

The theory behind this odd exterior decoration is rooted in the folklore and beliefs of a pre-Christian era. Visitors came to the well on the first Sunday in May (nowadays the custom continues all the year round) and took a drink of the water. At Craiguck Well at nearby Avoch, according to Sir Arthur Mitchell in his book *The Past in the Present* (1862), throngs of folk would arrive at the well before sunrise. Each would spill the water three times on the ground and cross himself before fixing a rag to a nearby bush. Then the person would drink the water. In drinking the water, those enjoying good health would hope to ensure that this continued. Those suffering from illness would leave behind a rag in the hope that whatever affliction they suffered from would be transferred, via the rag, to the sacred tree growing nearby.

The custom of leaving rags at the clootie well outside Munlochy is still practised with enthusiasm, judging by the amount of material on the surrounding bushes. The local tourist guide states that tradition dictates that anyone removing a rag will suffer the same misfortune as the original owner. But while in the past strands of natural fibres such as cotton, linen or wool would disintegrate in time, the same does not apply to much of the rags now left there, and several pairs of decaying tights do not go far in upholding an old and rather romantic tradition.

Munlochy, on the Black Isle, is about ten miles north of Inverness. Take the A9 northbound from Inverness for seven miles and then at the Tore roundabout turn right onto the A832. The Clootie Well is a couple of miles further on, to the right of the road.

The Blue Stane

It is not the usual reason for a visit to St Andrews, and it is almost totally ignored by the locals, but the Blue Stane (and you might have to clear the rubbish away from around it to see it properly) is older than most of the ecclesiastical, educational and golfing establishments for which St Andrews is famed.

The story of the Blue Stane, which is in fact more of a reddish sandstone colour, has its origins in the earliest history of St Andrews. Legend has it that an angry giant threw this substantial

Legend has it that an angry giant threw this chunk of sandstone at the missionary St Rule, one story even boasting that he threw it from Blebo Craigs, five miles distant!

block of sandstone at the missionary St Rule, who had usurped the giant's influence. However, legend also records that the giant was not one of life's bolder characters. He made sure that he remained far enough away from this upstart, St Rule, and threw the stone from the safe vantage point of Blebo Craigs, around five miles away.

The giant was to pay for his lack of courage. The stone landed short of its target and St Rule continued to flourish. The stone then became a trysting place, and a story goes that the local knights swore allegiance to the kings of Scotland over its rounded top, and the bold men of Fife rallied round the standard of Robert the Bruce before marching to Bannockburn. In later medieval times, and even up to the last century, stories abound of farmers patting the stone to bring them good luck at the market, and travellers would fondle it and hope for protection on their journeys.

One problem with the Blue Stane is that it was often on the move. First it lay somewhere on Magus Muir, near the site of the murder of Archbishop Sharpe, then between the First and Second World Wars it was located at the West Port before settling inside the railings of the Kate Kennedy Bar, opposite Hope Park Church.

No one pays it much attention now, and it is quite difficult to touch at all. But some of the world's top golfers might be wise to wend their way into the garden of the Kate Kennedy Bar and give it a little pat for luck.

St Andrews, Fife. Approach St Andrews from the A91, and turn right at the first roundabout. Continue on until a second roundabout. The Blue Stane is behind railings opposite Hope Park Church.

Unlucky stones

The small village of Rothiemurchus lies close by the ancient Comyn stronghold on Loch an Eilein, in which the notorious Wolf of Badenoch once lived. No great surprise then that the kirkyard contains the so-called Grave of the Curse, although the grave in question looks unprepossessing enough.

Above a flat slab are five odd stones, shaped like small bollards, which look as though they must have been used to support something. In all probability this would have been the gravestone above. The memorial stone at the head of these stones states that this is the resting place of Farquhar Shaw, who led thirty clansmen to the North Inch of Perth in 1596, where they defeated the Davidsons of Invernahaven. But this defeat seems to be nothing to do with the legend of the stones.

It is said that if any one of the stones is taken away from its site, the stone will find its way back to its stated place on the grave of its own accord and that within the year some disaster will befall the remover of the stone. A local story tells of the Duchess of Bedford, who in 1830 was holidaying at the House of Doune nearby. A servant of hers, one Robert Scroggie, took one of the stones and cast it into the river. When this act was discovered, he was told to find the stone and replace it immediately, but he drowned in the river a few days later.

There are tales of other visitors tempting fate and removing a stone. The result is always the same – the unfortunate visitor is invariably overcome by tragedy.

Rothiemurchus churchyard, Inverness-shire, is just south of Aviemore. From the south take the A9 to just a couple of miles south of Aviemore, where you should branch east onto the A951. Less than a mile further, take the B970 south for about one and a half miles until you see the entrance to Doune House, Doune Farm, and eventually the West Lodge to Doune Estate. Although the ruins of the church and graveyard are very close to the B970, they are partly obscured by trees and also on private ground. Those wishing to visit should ask at Doune House for permission.

The games at Glenisla

The Glenisla Highland Games take place almost at the northernmost end of the glen, on the west of the river. The field is bounded by the river on one side, with the road on the other, and the seating is carved out of the ground in turfs. It must be one of the most picturesque of all Highland Games grounds.

The games were founded in 1856, and came about because of the number of competitive heavyweight athletes in the glen. There was a lot of rivalry between these 'heavies', and being in such a remote and scattered area, they seldom managed to get together for a competitive trial of their respective strengths. So they decided to hold a games.

Local pipers and dancers, hearing of this decision, also decided to get in on the act, and as news of this proposed games day spread around, local landlords and the 'gentry' as well as glen folk arrived to see the fun. That first games was such a success that the Glenisla Highland and Friendly Society was formed. At that first games, the programme consisted of nine events, for which £13 was offered in prize money, while membership totalled ninety-four. Over a thousand people gathered to witness the contests.

There are curious twists in the annals of the games. At the first gathering three local pipers did duty, but by the following year, the dignity of the games demanded more. An official piper was engaged. His name was A. Abercrombie and he hailed from Braemar. The charges were carefully documented.

'Going for piper … 7*s*. 6*d*.' 'Hire 15*s*.'
(How he got home is a mystery.)
'Dinner and drink to a policeman 5*s*.' 'Candles for the ball 3*s*.'

The financial side of the Society was well protected. All the incomings were placed in the official coffers, with three separate locks, the President, Vice-President and Treasurer carrying a key each.

By 1859 Donald Dinnie, an outstanding all-round athlete, whose fame lived on for generations, came to compete in the games, but having won, was excluded by the rules of the Society from competing for three years afterwards. Between 1863 and 1865 Dinnie therefore was excluded from competing in the stone, hammer, caber, long leap, high leap, running and dancing, although he was still permitted to compete for the championship trophies.

Glenisla, Perthshire. The games field can be found on the west side of the River Isla on the B951 about three miles north of the Kirkton of Glenisla. Take the A93 north from Blairgowrie, turning off to Glenisla either on the secondary road east to Blacklunans or the B951 east to Glenisla.

Conical hill where the witches met Macbeth

This very strange-shaped hill lends itself naturally to a legend without any stage dressing. Rumour has it that this was the hill where Macbeth met the witches. Shakespeare referred to their meeting upon 'a blasted heath', and indeed the area of hill round about is fairly barren and heather-covered, and certainly the wind whips down Glenbran. Shakespeare, of course, never visited this area but it is a fitting setting for some words of fame from the Third Witch:

Be lion-mettled, proud, and take no care
Who chafes, who frets, or where conspirers are:

This curious conical hill looks a believable shape for a meeting place for witches, and indeed it is credited with being the spot where the three witches met Macbeth.

Macbeth shall never vanquish'd be until
Great Birnam wood to high Dunsinane hill
Shall come against him.

Abernyte, Perthshire. From Perth take the A90 to Dundee for about twelve miles, leaving to go north on the B953 at Inchture. Follow the B953 through Abernyte, taking a right turn about one mile after the village and keeping on this road for about one and a half miles until Lochton Farm is on the right, and a farm track leads to Glenbran Farm, on the left. Stop here, or carry on a few hundred yards. Both positions give a clear view of the conical-shaped hill to the west, about two miles away. Just south of this is the alleged fairy stronghold in the Sidlaws of Shian Hill. It is a noticeable hillock on the skyline, just south of Balbeggie. Nearby are traces of an ancient clachan, marked on the Ordnance Survey map, and known by the curious name of 'Bogle bee'.

Witches' pool

The Union Bridge at Keith, Moray, bears the inscription 'G.lll RR.S. 1770'. The bridge was widened in 1816 and partly rebuilt in 1912. But it is not the bridge which is awe-inspiring: it is the Gaun's Pool, which swirls below.

This deep pool was used for testing the guilt of suspected witches, who were flung into the pool from the south bank, from the appropriately named Gaun's Stone. There appeared to be little escape for these unfortunate women, for if they sank they were presumed to have been innocent, and if they floated were judged to be guilty and hauled out to be condemned to death.

Not far away, but now gone, was the gallows tree, where male criminals were punished. The story is told of one offender nailed to the tree by his ear to prevent escape, who wrenched himself free so that he might get a better view of a witch being drowned.

Keith is seventeen miles east of Elgin, on the A96.

The Union Bridge at Keith bears the inscription 'G.lll RR.S. 1770' and dramatically below swirls the Gaun's Pool, used for 'testing' or drowning local witches.

3

Trees, wooden shelters and wonderlands

Prickly memories

The life and work of Hugh MacDiarmid (1892–1978), poet, founder-member of the Scottish National Party, one-time Communist, and thorn in the flesh of the civic fathers of his native Langholm, is commemorated by a bronze memorial just outside the town, but without even a signpost from the A7.

He was born Christopher Murray Grieve, the son of a Langholm postman, and he became a much-acclaimed poet, gathering in an honorary degree from Edinburgh University with a citation which compared him to Thomas Carlyle and David Hume. However this cut no ice with his local town, the worthies of which he had antagonised by lampooning them unmercifully. So his funeral in Langholm churchyard was not attended by the local dignitaries, despite mourners flocking in from all around the world.

Perhaps a suitable finale to the saga of his memorial should be the plantation of a small garden of thistles in memory of his most famous poem, 'A Drunk Man Looks at the Thistle', written in 1926. The poem tells of a drunk man gradually coming to sobriety on a hillside and having to contend with the huge thistle that confronts him symbolically in the moonlight. This represented a gradually awaking spiritual awareness of what Scotland can be:

> The thistle rises and forever will,
> Getherin the generations under't.
> This is the monument o aa they were,
> And aa they hoped and wondered.

Langholm, Dumfries and Galloway, lies about fourteen miles north of Gretna on the A7.

Twin otters

Gavin Maxwell (1914–1969), author and naturalist among many other things, was brought up in Galloway. His most famous book, and the one with which his name is instantly associated, is the best-selling *Ring of Bright Water*, about life in his remote highland cottage with his otters and other animals.

The idea of a memorial to Gavin Maxwell came to John Davies, then the Forestry Commission conservator for southern Scotland, when he was to give a talk to the Galloway Association of Scotland. A group of people then spearheaded a fund-raising

Sculpture of a sleek bronze otter overlooking Luce Bay, at Monreith, Dumfries and Galloway, commemorates the birthplace nearby of Gavin Maxwell author of the modern classic *Ring of Bright Water*.

campaign to raise enough money to commission Penny Wheatley, a young Scots sculptor, to produce a bronze statue of an otter. This memorial now sits on a rock overlooking Luce Bay, close to Maxwell's birthplace of Monreith.

Penny Wheatley produced several ideas in preparation for this commission, and, anxious to make use of the statue that came a close second in choice for the original site, Mr Davies suggested another home for this second sculpture. He persuaded the Forestry Commission to place the unselected bronze otter in the 'Otter Pool' in Galloway Forest Park. The otter now watches over a popular natural swimming pool, ideal for children, where the water is shallow and children are never out of their depth, and rocky inlets afford an ideal otter play area.

Monreith, Dumfries and Galloway, is on the A747 about fourteen miles south-east of the main A75 Dumfries to Stranraer road. The Forestry Commission land, Galloway Forest Park, can be approached from the A762 south of New Galloway, or from the A712 Newton Stewart to New Galloway road. To find the otter statue, follow the signs to the 'Otter Pool'.

The John Knox tree

About the beginning of the twentieth century, the owner of Finlaystone in Renfrewshire, George Kidston, was left a widower, his wife having died after giving birth to their ninth child. To the rescue of this motherless troupe came George's sister, Miss Hamilton Kidston, who took charge of the children and the running of the household.

Miss Hamilton Campbell Kidston (or Aunty Bye as her brother's children succinctly called her) was profoundly interested in embroidery, and when Finlaystone was being altered by her brother, she seized her opportunity and hinted that she could do with a better light to sew by. Only too anxious to keep his vital housekeeper and proxy mother to his children as happy as possible, George built a bow window. George's window was of course the work of the architect, Sir John James Burnett, a contemporary of Charles Rennie Mackintosh. Why the window was placed in exactly this spot is conjecture. A bow window

In 1900 this yew tree was carefully transported 35 metres from where it originally stood. Under its branches John Knox celebrated his first Reformed Communion in the west of Scotland in 1556.

anywhere else would certainly have looked odd. All the same, it is hard to believe that it was not until the window was complete that George Kidston realised that John Knox's tree was blocking the light planned for Aunty Bye's embroidery work.

The John Knox tree was so named because it was reputed to occupy the spot where John Knox celebrated the first Reformed Communion in the west of Scotland in 1556. His patron was Alexander Cunningham, fifth Earl of Glencairn, one of the fifteen earls who held Finlaystone from the early fifteenth to the late eighteenth century.

The John Knox yew tree was, at the turn of the twentieth century, still in its prime and growing ever larger. Even then, it seems, the tree preservation lobby was active; or else Mr Kidston had a strong sense of history. He certainly seems to have had a healthy respect for timber. It is said that he was only once in his life seen to be really angry, and that was when he found some of his children shortening the legs of the drawing-room chairs with the aid of a saw. At all events he was most reluctant to fell the offending yew tree. The alternative was to move it. But no one in Britain seemed keen to transplant a tree that had supposedly survived nearly three and a half centuries – more, if it had been big enough for Knox to preach a sermon underneath it.

At last an American firm did the job, as the photographs show. Thanks to a trench, some railway lines and a team of horses, the yew now grows about thirty-five meters south-west of where it stood in 1900. In 1943 Hitler tried to rectify its easterly list by dropping a bomb about forty-five meters to the south-east; but he failed to make much impression. Recently the tree has developed a brown patch at its crown, enough to remind us that even the days of a tree are numbered.

Finlaystone is on the A8 about ten miles west of Glasgow airport. The grounds are open to the public all year.

Crowned with leaves

The small wood above Kingarth Hotel at the south end of the Isle of Bute can be seen distinctly from the Bruchag Road. The trees were planted in 1948 to commemorate the birth of a famous man. Other clues might include his royal status and the name of the nearest town. A last clue can be gleaned from the shape of the plantation – a crown.

ANSWER: A grove of trees in the shape of a crown was planted to commemorate the birth of Prince Charles, whose premier title in Scotland is Duke of Rothesay.

Rothesay, Isle of Bute. The Kingarth Hotel is about eight miles south of Rothesay on the A844.

The 'Heart of Scotland' too is commemorated by trees, and placed right in the very centre of the country. South of Aberfeldy, Perthshire, and adjacent to the walk of the Birks of Aberfeldy, is a small wood which from the air is the shape of a heart. Measuring just under a quarter of a mile across, the distinct shape is most easily viewed on an Ordnance Survey map.

Abriachan, by Drumnadrochit

Blinker yourself to the regimented Sitka spruce trees at Abriachan. Imagine you are creeping along around 1500 BC, treading stealthily in case a wolf, bear or lynx lies close by. Then, safety awaits round the corner, or at least that is what any roofed structure feels like to us, no matter if that structure is fairly flimsy. Ahead, partially camouflaged, glimpsed in revealing stages, is an authentic Bronze Age hut, circular with a conical roof. This surprise is but one of those to be found at the Abriachan Community Forest.

Taking the steep road up from the main Loch Ness road, a journey of five miles brings you to this fairly well concealed oasis. The imaginative walkways, sculptures, decking over the loch allowing wheelchair-bound birdwatchers direct access, an ark built in the trees and a bothy constructed a couple of miles up as a place of shelter on the open moorland are even more impressive if you realise that this was a local community forest buy-out, spearheaded by the local shepherd's wife.

Every member of this remote and scattered community was involved, and perhaps most unusual of all is the triumph created by the area's teenagers, the replica Bronze Age hut. The idea won them an award which whisked them off to view Masai huts in Africa. Inside, once your eyes have become accustomed to the gloom, you can see the branched doors and sheepskin rugs and get a sense of life as it was lived thousands of years ago.

One of the largest community-owned woodlands in the UK, encompassing 534 hectares, this extensive area of land was purchased by local folk in 1998, when it was named the Abriachan Forest Trust. The Trust now proudly claims to have planted 100,000 native trees to replace commercially grown conifers.

The Trust area encloses Loch Laide, and opens out onto extensive heather-clad hilly ground above the tree line. Signs carved from oak have hinged pointers to various paths, and interpretation posts have information on birds and animals found in the vicinity and on their calls. We are many centuries on from the days when the woodlands in this area sheltered folk within structures hand-wrought from local materials and the Bronze Age dwelling gives the closest approximation to just what it must have felt like living within a flimsy hut.

To find the Abriachan Forest Trail, travelling from Inverness, take the A82 south for Fort William. After four miles you will see the first signpost marked for Blackfold and Abriachan. Do not take this, but continue for a further four miles and take the right turn marked Abriachan at the large turning circle.

In Abriachan: travel up the Abriachan road for about a mile and the village hall is the grey corrugated iron building on your right. Shortly after the hall there is a junction; take the left fork, marked Abriachan Forest Walks. Passing a small loch on your left, the Abriachan Forest is the next left turn. The Forest Trust car park is 300 metres on the left.

Fairy grotto within a fairy glen

Once upon a time, the grotto just beside the Reelig Glen Forest Walk must have inspired the ladies of Reelig House and their admirers to sit and muse within its walls. It was built in 1850 in a style which appealed to the then owner of the estate, James Baillie Fraser. It is partly ruined now, a state of affairs not inappropriate to the mystery surrounding the naming of this 'Fairy Glen'.

Apparently many hours each day were spent building up the grotto but by the following morning it was once more reduced to a pile of stones. The locals therefore named the glen after the fairies who, they said, must have spent their nights pulling down the work of man. The truth might not be so other-worldly, but it does suggest much about the generosity and kindliness of the then laird.

At that time the infamous Highland Clearances were drawing to a close, during which thousands of crofters were evicted from the land they had farmed for centuries to make way for the new age of sheep. Many came to the area round Reelig, homeless and penniless, looking for employment. James Baillie Fraser must have been a kinder laird than many of his Highland contemporaries, for he paid the men the sum of 9*d*. per day to work in his woods. The story goes that those building grottos and paths found that there was always more work; however much they built in one day, the next morning it had been pulled down and they had to start again. The story at the time was that the fairies of the glen were responsible for undoing their work, but others said that Fraser himself went out at night to pull down the stonework so that there would always be enough work to keep the men employed.

Reelig Forest Walk, in the care of the Forestry Commission, is eight miles west of Inverness on the south side of the A862 Inverness to Beauly road. Leave the A862 by the road signposted Moniack and Clunes.

Kingston

The large village of Kingston, Moray, hides a timber-laden story, for it was here in 1785 that two enterprising Englishmen from Kingston-upon-Hull came to start a ship-building business. (The spot had enjoyed a brief previous claim to fame, when Charles II landed on the shore at Garmouth on 23 June 1650, swearing to abide by the National Covenant and the Solemn League and Covenant immediately before coming ashore.)

The reasoning of the Yorkshiremen was simple enough. Several types of timber suitable for ship-building were readily available within the forests of the Spey. They established a settlement and a rapidly thriving business which at its zenith produced ships of up to 700 tons, much larger than those produced at either Perth or Dundee. The business grew into seven yards, building up to 300 ships. Among these ships were famous clippers and Cape Horners. John Duncan of Garmouth, one of the leading shipowners in the nineteenth century, had his office in what was called Red Corb House. (A corb or corf was a basket, usually made from iron.)

Two factors led to the demise of these famous ship-building yards: the arrival of iron ships, which superseded wood, and the ever-changing mouth of the Spey. Today, the area once the scene of busy shipyards has vanished, covered by acres of stones, driven down the Spey when in spate.

Kingston, Moray, is on the changing mouth of the Spey on the west bank. It is about five miles north of Fochabers, on the B9015.

Arbroath pippin

'This is an excellent apple; as to flavour it is outdone by none but the Nonpareil, over which it has this advantage, that it will ripen in a worse climate and a worse aspect.' So said Walter Nicol, a nineteenth-century authority on fruit and the kitchen garden.

The apple to which he was referring, the Arbroath pippin, certainly needed to be able to withstand bad weather, as it either originated in the Arbroath area or might have been brought over from the softer climes of middle France by the monks who settled at Arbroath in the twelfth century.

The apple has a curious habit. The branches are covered with knobs or burrs, which, when planted in the ground, throw out numerous fibres which take root and produce a perfect tree. Dr Robert Hogg, a noted nineteenth-century pomologist reported that:

> the fruit is a pale yellow colour and thickly strewed with brown dots, very frequently cracked, forming large and deep clefts in the fruit. The flesh is yellowish, firm, crisp and juicy, rich and sweet with a highly aromatic flavour which is particular to this apple only. In the *Jardinier François*, which was published in 1651, I find the apple mentioned under the name of Orgeran, which is so similar in pronunciation to Orgeline, I think that not unlikely it may be the same name with a change of orthography, especially as our ancestors were not over particular in preserving unaltered the names of foreign introductions.

One lone example of this curious Arbroath relict still exists. It is on the front lawn of the Scottish Crop Research Institute at Invergowrie, three miles west of Dundee.

Just east of the Invergowrie Main Street roundabout, turn south off the A90 and follow signs to the Scottish Crop Research Institute, about half a mile from the turn-off.

The Shakespeare tree

The Shakespeare tree which lies in the grounds of Kemnay House is not reputed to have been planted by William Shakespeare himself – or any such unlikely story. In fact this enormous beech was planted around 200 years ago by an ancestor of a more recent occupier of Kemnay House, Mrs Susan Burnett of Kemnay. George Burnett was a noted horticulturalist and agriculturalist of the eighteenth century, and Mrs Burnett pointed out that the grounds and avenues here were among the finest in Scotland.

The tree's association with Shakespeare came about in 1923 through the enthusiasm of the newly appointed headmaster of Kemnay Secondary School, Mr Minto Robertson. Along with his English teacher at the school, Miss Henderson, Mr Robertson produced a Shakespeare play every year for about forty years, the stage being under the tree.

Mrs Burnett recalled that:

the plays were performed at the end of June every year, and we only repaired to the public hall if the weather broke down. I am not certain, but I think this happened only once in forty-odd years. The whole school was involved with the production, if not in performing parts then in making tickets and posters and making certain 'props'. The acting was of an extremely high standard and prompting practically unheard of. A love of Shakespeare was passed on to all those taking part, and when it came to our Highers, none of us had any qualms about the questions on Shakespeare plays. We could quote several by heart. The tree itself provided a wonderful backdrop and auditorium, its branches spreading over the first rows of the audience as well. The main worry was the midges, which were and are of a very energetic strain.

Kemnay, Aberdeenshire, is about sixteen miles from Aberdeen on the A96 and then the B993.

Standing to attention

When Mr Husband of Glenearn, in Perthshire, purchased his estate, he immediately set about the task of upgrading his property. There was nothing exceptional in that, as in the early part of the nineteenth century new owners liked nothing better than to ennoble their surroundings. Thus he moved from the cramped old laird's house under the shadow of the nearby hills and built a fine white-painted Palladian house on the crest of a small hill, and planted trees alongside the new sweeping drives. He chose a spot easily visible to the passing traveller on the Perth to Edinburgh highway.

When this building was completed in a style sufficiently elegant to impress the neighbours, Mr Husband turned his patriotic attentions to the planting of the hill which formed a splendid backdrop to his new house. Travellers would gaze across at the symmetrical planting that was taking place, but with a touch of puzzlement. Mr Husband planted up his hills like a scenic stage backdrop for his house, but his intentions were, and still are, obvious only to the initiated. In fact, the trees were planted to grow in the military formations of the Battle of Waterloo – the British side, of course. The yews, beech trees and firs are gathered in tight and formidable ranks at the foot of Glenearn Hill, and higher up are smaller, neater circles of trees still referred to as the Indian Woods, supposedly after the Sepoy battalions they represent. History seems to have been ignored in this naming, as there does not appear to be any record of Indian soldiers fighting at Waterloo, the battle taking place before Indian soldiers joined the ranks of any British army.

Meanwhile down at the old laird's house, Ecclesiamagirdle (pronounced Exmagriddle), Mr Husband dammed the burn to make a trout loch, cutting it out in the shape of Great Britain. Ecclesiamagirdle still exists with its ruined church and graveyard containing the tomb of the first Covenanter to die. Much of the loch's shape is blurred by reeds, but you can still stand on top of Indian Hill and peer down upon a small acre of water that was intended to be forever Great Britain.

Other woody Waterloos supposedly exist in Scotland. Unconfirmed examples of woods planted out in the same spirit are to be found near Loch Striven in Argyll, on a promontory at the eastern entrance to the Kyles of Bute, and at Wellington's Pillar near Jedburgh, where the surrounding forestry, as one might expect, is said to echo the famous battle-lines.

Glenearn, by Bridge of Earn, Perthshire. One place to pick out this arboreal battle plan is when coming over the crest of the hill at Friarton just south of Perth on the M90: the outlines can just be distinguished. The low line of trees stands just behind the white Regency house of Glenearn, which often gleams in the sunshine and makes it easier to pick out the battle-lines above.

Another view of the trees can be seen, and is easiest picked out when snow outlines them rather well, by turning off west on a side road, the B935 from Bridge of Earn to Forgandenny. However, the pond, Ecclesiamagirdle and the graveyard are in private ownership and contact would have to be made with the owners of Glenearn House.

The wall and the minister's pulpit

The following contemporary account, written at the end of the nineteenth century, describes the scene at an outdoor church service at Shieldaig in Wester Ross:

It was nearly two o'clock before we arrived at Shieldaig. A large congregation had been waiting for nearly two hours but this is thought nothing of in the Highlands. Here was another scene like that at Applecross. The tent was placed amidst the naked rocks on the sea shore – the sound of the psalms literally mingled with the roar of the waves of the Atlantic. The tent was fastened down with strong ropes to prevent its being upset, and there were grey-headed men sitting uncovered in the cold and several of them with tears streaming down their cheeks whilst Mr Glass [the minister] preached to them the blessed Gospel in their native tongue. Every new spectacle I witnessed deepened my impression of astonishment. Close beside where this interesting congregation assembled was a government church and manse which have been shut up since the Disruption, there being only one 'Moderate' in the whole district. This church, built with

During disagreements between landowners and tenants in the nineteenth century, Communion services were often held outdoors, with worshippers waiting hours for the preachers to arrive. This photograph shows a congregation near Plockton.

public money, is actually locked up whilst the poor Highlanders must face all the storms of winter on the bare sea beach, they being here also denied a single inch of land on which to erect a place of worship. Such a state of matters in Ireland would soon shake the empire, and it is Christian principle alone which has borne it so meekly in our land. We were told here by the Catechist, a worthy and somewhat picturesque looking man called in Gaelic 'White John', that there had lately been a revival of vital godliness in the district especially amongst the young, and produced by instrumentality of reading the word of God and the whole aspect of the congregation bore evident works of the power of the spirit of God.

The village sits on Loch Torridon on the A896, at the edge of the Applecross peninsula. The history of the church in the area is typical of the vicissitudes which small congregations suffered after the Disruption of 1843.

Around this time, a sheltering wall was built in order to shield the congregation from the sea winds, and this still stands, to the

FREE CHURCH COMMUNION, PLOCKTON.

north of the village. Known as the Cos (Gaelic for a hollow) it rises two metres high. The area was in use for many years as an open preaching place after the Disruption in 1843 when the Free Church broke away, and again after 1892 when the Free Presbyterian Church broke away from the Free Church.

At some point during this latter time the minister's tent was replaced with a wooden pulpit, rather like a large sentry box with a flap which rose to allow the minister to stand inside but left his head and shoulders visible to the congregation.

In the first quarter of this century, after a church had been built, the wooden pulpit was still used. During the times of the twice-yearly Communion, in the spring and autumn, large gatherings of people would attend. This meant that the numbers were too great to fit into the church and therefore the services were held outside.

The wooden pulpit to be seen in the Gairloch Museum came from Shieldaig, a reminder of the hardships which the people of the area endured until the twentieth century.

Gairloch Museum is situated on the A832 near the Tourist Information Centre in Gairloch, Wester Ross.

Shieldaig is on the A896 about twenty-six miles north of Kyle of Lochalsh.

4

Secret arts and crafted to amuse

Catherine Sinclair (1800–1864)

The fountain erected by novelist and philanthropist Catherine Sinclair at the junction of Lothian Road and Princes Street in Edinburgh proved such a popular landmark that it caused disruption to the thoroughfare and had to be moved. This was the first drinking fountain in the city, and had cups for people to quench their thirst as well as troughs at a lower level for horses and dishes at the base for dogs to lap from. It was a fitting memorial for someone who cared deeply for the oppressed and poor, but she was also a best-selling author, a celebrity in her day and revered by many.

Upon her death in London in 1864 Miss Sinclair's body was carried home to Edinburgh to be buried, the cortège resting on the journey while crowds gathered to pay their respects to her. She is buried in Edinburgh, in the vaults of St John's Episcopal Church, on the corner of Princes Street and Lothian Road.

Catherine Sinclair was the daughter of Sir John Sinclair, and one of thirteen children. Despite being from a large family, the children flourished intellectually, as one might expect of the offspring of the man who initiated the Statistical Accounts of Scotland. Her father was also the first President of the Board of Agriculture.

Catherine was her father's secretary from the age of fourteen, and then became an author in her own right. She wrote prolifically and very successfully: in her lifetime she published thirty-seven books ranging in subject matter from humorous attacks on female education, or lack of it, to travel books chronicling her journeys throughout the UK. She is credited with being the first person to guess the identity of the author of the Waverley Novels. She hired public halls and persuaded her literary and scientific friends to give lectures. One of her books, *Beatrice*, was apparently a better seller than *Uncle Tom's Cabin*. Many of her books for children are now forgotten, but the most famous was *Holiday House* (1839).

Catherine Sinclair also devoted much time to good works. Indeed, she commented upon her writing that 'of all the paper I have blotted, I have written nothing without the intention of some good'. She was the first to introduce soup kitchens for the poor workers in Leith; she organised the Volunteer Brigade in Leith, a forerunner of the Boys Brigade, which came into being twenty years after her death; she maintained a large school to prepare girls for domestic service; and she erected the first of the cab stands so that cab drivers could shelter out of the worst of the weather while waiting to ply their trade. But fame is fickle and popularity and memories can dissipate rapidly. Hence not one copy of her books is currently in print or available in public libraries for borrowing, only as reference.

Hopetoun House, Tyninghame House, the McLaren Wing and Cardenden: William McLaren, muralist from Cardenden

Pick up Dawn MacLeod's classic account of the famous gardens at Inverewe, Argyll, *Oasis of the North*, and there is Willie McLaren, his flamboyant drawings decorating the frontispiece. Peek into 29 Denfield Avenue, an unprepossessing council house in Cardenden, Fife, and you will see, covering an entire wall in an upstairs bedroom, an exuberant mural of a fifteenth-century party with twentieth-century guests, painted in the 1940s by Willie McLaren, a miner's son. His transformation of a section of Tyninghame House is immortalised as the McLaren Wing, and his depiction of classical scenes rising up the staircase at Hopetoun House are on view to visitors.

Born in 1923 with crippling deformities in both feet, he was a misfit at school due to his inability to play football and his prodigious early talent for drawing and painting. Encouraged by his mother, he won first a place at Edinburgh College of Art and the Andrew Grant Scholarship of £80 in 1940. After gaining his diploma in 1944, as well as a further highly commended post-diploma award in the following year, he went on to win a clutch of bursaries and scholarships. Then in 1945 came the Andrew Grant Easter Vocation Bursary of £10, and from the same source a travelling scholarship of £150 – a substantial sum at that time. With this in his pocket he left the grey skies of Fife in April and visited Florence, Rome and Sicily, as well as areas of France with which he also fell in love.

Returning home he decorated just about everything within reach in his house in Cardenden, and attacked his bedroom under the inspiration of the Tuscan sun, the Tuscan landscape and Italian Renaissance art. Glancing through the huge legacy he left behind in the way of illustrations and murals, it is clear that this critical early experience of the sun and the vitality of the Mediterranean way of life retained its effect on his outlook on life and on his art.

What is remarkable is that he returned from his life-changing trip to Italy and settled back at Cardenden, living quietly with his family, initially misunderstood by the Fife village-folk who thought only manual work counted. At home, he continued to decorate walls while waiting for paid work to come his way. It did. He was commissioned by the BBC to draw hundreds of illustrations for the *Radio Times*, and went on to illustrate over 600 books for what he referred to as his 'bread and butter' money. Most followed his much-loved classical forms. He remained true to such images, deeply unfashionable in the 1950s and '60s, to the end of his life, and used them in murals and in illustrations and in commissions for clients and friends of completely different backgrounds. His gifts for local Fife weddings were generous of time and skill. How many sideboards have an engraved piece of glass, done specially by Willie to depict the unique character of the recipient? When the local juvenile pipe bands won the world championship, Willie prepared elaborate scrolls for each of the nineteen junior members, proudly finished off with a scarlet seal stamped with a thistle. Even the stamp he made himself.

McLaren's *trompe-l'oeil* paintings covering the panels of the main staircase at Tyninghame were done at the same time as wedding presents of engraving on glass for every local friend in

Willie McLaren was an unlikely champion of the baroque style of drawing and painting, and came from an even more unlikely background – a coal-mining village in Fife.

Cardenden. Commissions varied hugely. He was responsible for the frontispiece for the Inverewe Gardens guide as well as for decorated furniture commissioned by Jimmy Thomson of A. F. Drysdale, the Edinburgh interior decorators, who recalled of him:

> Well, of course he was a born entertainer. In fact, he was a frustrated theatrical decorator, and he adored bright colours and extravagant decoration. He 'marbled' things long before this style of imitation rose to fashion again. He marbled items though, not in true imitation of real marble, but in bright raspberry pink, for example – sometimes you had to keep a really sharp eye on him, as this wasn't what many of the clients had in mind! And later he worked in continual chaos, always far too much work at once, or none at all.

On the occasions though when work or payment wasn't forthcoming, Willie was gloriously undeterred. He would sell off small items he had picked up in junk shops and to which he had applied his own individualistic paint style.

Classical Italian Renaissance art and baroque exuberance characterise
Willie McLaren's work. This painting in Wemyss Church, Fife, illustrates
one aspect of his prodigious talent.

Every single surface of his Edinburgh flat was painted in *trompe-l'oeil*, and his dog Farouche was famous for wearing a scarf instead of a collar. When Willie was too busy to take him out for a walk, Farouche took himself off alone. He made a regular trip on the bus down from his master's Edinburgh flat in Northumberland Place to Leith Walk from where he would wend his way back on foot, inspecting all the rubbish bins of the many restaurants on the return trip.

Farouche predeceased Willie, dying a few months before Willie's own death in October 1987. And there William McLaren's output might have been forgotten: such as his Christmas scenes painted on holidays in the sunny Mediterranean, holidays he enjoyed, regarding them as a reward to himself for his efforts with his 'bread and butter' workload; the

600 books he illustrated; the hundreds of covers for the *Radio Times*; and the exuberantly *trompe-l'oeil* walls of one of his Edinburgh flats. Somewhere may still lurk the many vibrantly decorated cardboard boxes he would transform into treasure chests for children.

But then, in 1989, Tom Kirk of Cardenden, who had known Willie of old, decided that he should be recognised, and put on an exhibition of his paintings in the Bowhill Miner's Institute, followed by three nights in the Ex-Servicemen's Club in Cardenden. He unearthed glass and scrolls, he discovered that the mural at 29 Denfield Avenue still existed behind the wallpaper. Finally, the folk of Cardenden viewed the output of a local lad. 'What a talented man,' wrote one visitor in the guest book. 'I had always thought he was such a lazy devil'!

Cardenden, Fife. Cardenden is on the B981 about four miles north-east of Cowdenbeath.

Tyninghame House, which is privately owned, is close the village of the same name, on the A198, seven miles east of Haddington.

Willie McLaren's murals can be seen on the main staircase at Hopetoun House, Edinburgh. Directions to Hopetoun House from central Edinburgh, approximately twelve miles: take the A90 for the Forth Road Bridge and the north. Just before the bridge take the slip road and turn left onto the A904. Approximately half a mile along this road turn right into South Queensferry. Directly under the road bridge there is a sign to Hopetoun House.

Buddhas and the earls of Buchan

Delgatie, by Turriff, is a traditional Z-plan castle dating from about 1030. It was home to the Hays of Delgatie, who snatched ownership from the Earl of Buchan around 1314 after the earl backed the wrong side in the Battle of Bannockburn. The castle, like so many ancient strongholds, has had a chequered past. With only one gap, it was owned and occupied by the Hay family from Bannockburn to 1997, when the castle and grounds came under the ownership of a trust. Mary, Queen of Scots stayed there after the Battle of Corrichie in 1562 and the visitor can see her bedroom. The turnpike stair of ninety-seven treads is reputed to be one of the widest in Scotland, and the original painted ceilings, which date from 1592 and 1597, are some of the country's finest. Some of the portraits are thought to represent the actual inhabitants of the time.

What the sixteenth-century Hays would think of the various Buddhas found in niches on the staircase, or the supporting walls for the garden using hundreds of empty spirit bottles, is anyone's guess. Indeed the more traditional guardians of our castles might be squirming at visions of eastern promise scattered about the fortress. It must be the most idiosyncratic clan stronghold in Scotland.

Who was behind these surprising additions? It was another Hay, this time an army captain, who bought the castle on a whim, using every penny he possessed, just after the Second World War, when the castle had been more or less condemned as past repair and was within a whisker of having its roof stripped off. Coming from a long line of Indian Army soldiers, Hay was a soldier through and through, but possessed a useful skill not normally associated with soldiering. He was a skilled stonemason, a skill acquired from years of making do in the isolated Indian provinces. Captain Hay made heroic efforts not only to restore the buildings but also to construct concrete ponds, holding areas for water in case of fire, intricate damming systems, circular stone herb gardens, and everywhere are carved initials, designs set into concrete and inserted into walls and cobbled courtyards.

There are ghosts aplenty, as well as mementos of a rich past. The loch is fed through a series of cut stone channels constructed by soldiers returning from the Battle of Waterloo. The castle has also re-established vital links with Hays from around the world, and now hosts the Hay Clan gatherings and is open to the public from Easter to October.

After Captain Hay died in 1997, at the age of ninety-two and childless, he left the castle to the very proper hands of the Delgatie Castle Trust. Mrs Joan Johnson, Captain Hay's housekeeper for many years, now runs the castle, copes with several holiday cottages and flats within the castle, bakes all the homemade goodies for teas and snacks available for castle visitors, cleans everywhere, weeds much of the garden and is years past retirement age.

If you ever want to visit a place which is one man's dream, this is it.

Delgatie Castle, by Turriff, Aberdeenshire. From Banff take the A947 Aberdeen road south eleven miles and follow signposting for Delgatie Castle.

Sundials

'Scotland has a far greater recorded number of complex 17th- and 18th-century sundials than other countries.' So stated the late Andrew Somerville, whose great interest in sundials culminated in a comprehensive book on the subject.

Scotland is indeed scattered with sundials, remarkable on at least two counts. Firstly, they are very early pieces of carved stone which have somehow survived long after the spread of affordable clocks; and secondly, there is the mystery of their proliferation in Scotland, compared with other European countries.

Why were so many sundials produced here? Various theories have been propounded. The sixteenth century was a time of new ideas on construction, Renaissance attitudes were spreading, there was a keen interest in garden design and in the study and appreciation of science, and flung into this mix was the Calvinist movement which despised the frivolity of decoration for its own sake. All these attitudes stimulated the construction of items such as sundials. Although the original designs of sundials came from Germany, each country adapted its own theories and Scotland developed new sundial faces.

One craftsman who founded in the seventeenth century a small masonic dynasty was a Perthshire stonemason named John Mylne. The masonic movement also influenced the increasingly elaborate designs and new types of faces. Andrew Somerville concluded that the emergence of a unique freemasonry at this time coincided with inimitable, highly sophisticated and elaborate sundial construction.

Sundials enjoyed a heyday of around two centuries before abruptly disappearing in the mid-eighteenth century, when their

Scotland possessed a far greater recorded number of complex 17th- and 18th-century sundials than most other countries. This one stands proud outside Glamis Castle.

design zenith seems to have peaked. By then, Scotland was entering the age of Industrial Revolution and money was being made by a different class of people whose interest swayed towards things mechanical.

Elaborate clocks became available, incorporating astronomical, tidal and equation dials and, it must be said, they could be read by the owner in the comfort of his increasingly comfortable home. Who would blame him for preferring such toys? Especially when his guests could not avoid noticing and admiring them in their eye-catching positions on a prominent plinth in his hall.

Sundials were to enjoy isolated and sporadic revivals. One is taking place now, at the turn of the twenty-first century, though their use is generally purely ornamental. Ian Hamilton Finlay, the Scottish poet, sculptor and gardener who died in March 2006, made modern sundials into his own art form, but at the beginning of the twentieth century architects such as Sir Robert Lorimer commissioned sundials in 'the old style' to match the restoration of a castle.

There were three main styles of sundial: the lectern shape, the obelisk shape and the facet-headed.

The lectern shape usually resembles the classic Bible-supporting lectern, with the copper gnomons (the slice of metal which casts the shadow) set into different sides of the stone block, so that as the sun moves round, the time can be read on different faces during the day.

An adaptation of the lectern style is the moon and tidal dial. Four of these still in existence are known to be the work of John Bonar, master at Ayr Grammar School from 1612 to 1638. All are inscribed with the names of ports and would have had movable arms to set to the phases of the moon so that they could be used as moon dials and also for predicting the time of high tide.

The obelisk dial seems to be unique to Scotland. The basic shape is pierced with elaborate bowl hollows, hearts or rectangular shapes, with many dials and gnomons. Only twenty-five complete dials of this type are still known to exist. They were more fragile than the sturdy lectern shape, and if the upper part was knocked off, they were liable to be rebuilt incorrectly.

The many facet-headed dials appear in a wide variety of shapes, and with strikingly flamboyant decoration. One of the most famous of this type is the one at Glamis Castle, and one of the finest is at the Palace of Holyrood, made for the Scottish coronation of Charles I in 1633 by the famous master mason John Mylne.

An adaptation of this type of dial could show the time in a number of cities around the world; the one at Nunraw Abbey, in East Lothian, has dials for twenty-two cities as well as the local time.

These assorted styles of sundials, part of Scotland's unique heritage, can be viewed in the grounds of several houses open to the public by the National Trust for Scotland (e.g. Castle Fraser and Haddo House, both in Aberdeenshire; Culzean, South Ayrshire) as well as at stately homes, such as Glamis, Angus, and in the grounds of several houses open to the public under Scotland's Gardens Scheme (SGS).

The church that set sail

The Buckhaven Theatre presents many assorted plays within its walls, telling of stories both realistic and far-fetched, but few can be as strange as the story of the building itself, and of its transformation from church to theatre.

From its exterior appearance, the front presents a bold example of Victorian architecture and confidence, as indeed it might, the 1853 façade being the work of the noted architect Sir Gilbert Scott. However, the building was erected earlier, designed by another well-known architect, William Burn. The foundation stone was laid on 27 August 1824, and the completed church was consecrated by the bishop on 29 September 1825. Less than fifty years after the foundation stone was laid, the building was uprooted and transported from its original site in St Andrews to Buckhaven.

The building was situated originally on the north side of North Street, St Andrews, in part of the university gardens of today and a little to the west of the graduation hall. Why and how it moved to Buckhaven is a simple tale of supply and demand. It was put up for sale in 1870, at the same time as the Free Church in Buckhaven was gathering money into their building fund for the construction of a new church. The Buckhaven congregation were making use of an old school at the time and the seating was insufficient for their average Sunday attendance of 250. So when they heard about the Episcopal Church in St Andrews being for sale, they inspected it, found it to their satisfaction and paid £130 for it, which was considerably less than the £236 in cash within their coffers, plus the £300 already promised them by subscribers.

Slate by slate and stone by stone, the original building was dismantled, carefully marked and transported by carrier to the harbour at St Andrews, where it was transferred to a vessel, the *Sea*

The church that set sail. St Andrew's Church originally stood in St Andrews, but was transported stone by stone down the coast to Buckhaven, where it has stood there ever since.

King. This boat, owned by Messrs Thomas, William and John Walker, can have carried few stranger loads, but it arrived safely, and the re-constructed church now stands proudly on the site where it was rebuilt and dedicated in 1872. No record of stones disappearing or accidents seems to have emerged, but the storm which caused the Tay Rail Bridge to collapse in 1879 took its toll on the church. The cross which crowned the apex of the front of the church was blown down, to be replaced with an ornamental pinnacle.

The church is now converted into a theatre. The concept behind its conversion from little-used church hall – which is what the church had become after the amalgamation of the Church of Scotland churches in Buckhaven – was to help the depressed and unemployed.

Buckhaven is on the A955 in south Fife, eight miles north-east of Kirkcaldy and about thirteen miles south-west of St Andrews.

Underground art

Hard, black and very formal, the garden seat sits now in the garden of Osborne House, on the Isle of Wight; it was purchased by Prince Albert and exhibited at the Great Exhibition of 1851. Made by Thomas Williamson of West Wemyss (1817–1860), it is carved neither from a black wood, nor from marble or stone, but from a substance native to south Fife. Other examples of the creative carving of Thomas Williamson – and he managed to pack in a great deal into his short life – are on display in Kirkcaldy Museum, where the secret is revealed. They are carved from coal.

This particular coal is 'parrot coal', which was found in the Wemyss coalfields and further south in Fife at Torrie, as well as in many other areas throughout the UK. Generally mined from higher seams, the coal is very high in bitumen content, and is also

Shiny, black furniture made from coal was popular in Victorian times. The coal was polished to such an extent that it became clean enough to sit on and eat from.

able to be extracted in large blocks which do not split easily. When burnt it emits a very bright flame, but when carved and polished to a very high gloss, it takes on the appearance of shiny black marble.

Given the fondness of the Victorians for dark furniture, their emphasis on elaborate carving, and the vitality of an era which fostered exaggerated notions of decoration, why should we wonder at coal-carving? Odd as we may regard this type of carving today, as mystifying is the name of the coal. Parrot coal was thought to be named after the clicking of the bird's beak, which resembled the noise the burning coal emitted. This is a tale which lacks substance, popular as the keeping of parrots was in the nineteenth century. As early as 1693, the inventory at Rossie House, Forfar, noted '12 doz. Parrot coal'. This was listed with other household items, such as furniture, clocks and linen. It is described as being part of a wedding present given to Margaret Scott, formerly of Rankeillour, Cupar, Fifeshire, by her uncle, Sir James Weems.

How did Thomas Williamson, the son of a collier, become carver of coal seats which ended up in the royal gardens? In all probability Williamson started his working life down the pit, but at some point he carved an item with such skill that he drew the attention of Rear-Admiral James Erskine Wemyss of Wemyss and Torrie (1789–1854). The admiral commissioned several items of furniture from Williamson, and in effect became an influential patron. The wealth which the coalfields brought to him as a mine-owner would have also raised his social standing, and it was he who brought the products of Williamson to the attention of Prince Albert.

Williamson also carved items of jewellery, the sombre blackness of the coal being an ideal substitute for jet jewellery which enjoyed a widespread vogue throughout the Victorian era. He also was responsible for the carving of a tombstone in the churchyard of St Adrian's, West Wemyss.

Williamson's death certificate details his trade as being a 'journeyman mason'. His fame seems almost totally limited to a display in Kirkcaldy Museum based on his coal furniture. The curious part of this is that he was obviously not a trained furniture maker. His chairs, for instance, have no joints in the conventional or traditional sense, although they are all functional pieces. He made many items for Wemyss Castle, and a very formal set of table and chairs, made in 1855, was presented to the Kirkcaldy Museum in 1953 by Captain Wemyss of Wemyss Castle. The swan of the Weymss heraldic crest is carved on the chair under the words 'Je pense'. Almost unknown they may be, but as an example of enterprise and natural talent which was spotted, encouraged and exploited by the local laird, these rare curiosities are well worth the pride of place they have in the museum.

Though Thomas Williamson was the most notable carver of coal in the area, there were others. The *Fife Free Press* of 19 April 1890 wrote in its local news column from Dysart that a William Hunter, who died at the age of thirty, had spent the leisure hours of nine years of his life carving a 'highly ornamental mirror and dressing table' from one solid block of parrot coal which had been exhibited in Dundee Museum before being given to his mother. She later moved to Galashiels, where in 1890 the items were put up for sale. Another carver was also a Dysart resident, Allan Stewart (1833–1884), who, when not employed as a plasterer and model-maker, made small items such as a model tower or a brooch.

Kirkcaldy, Fife, lies about fourteen miles east of the M90, leaving at Junction 1 or Junction 3. Kirkcaldy Museum and Art Gallery is a minute's walk south of Kirkcaldy railway station.

Robert Morrison, monumental mason

The extensive Trinity Cemetery in Aberdeen can have few more poignant works of carving than the tombstone of Anne Morrison who died in 1930. She was forty when she died and the mother of seven children, one of whom followed her to the grave shortly afterwards. Her death at such an early age, and with so many young children, was indeed tragic. Her memorial eclipses in eloquence those round about. It was carved by her husband, Robert, whose achievements as a monumental mason may one day be more widely recognised.

The early death of the wife of Robert Morrison, a master carver from Aberdeen, inspired him with his greatest challenge in the form of this memorial obelisk to her.

Even in his own day, his skill and speed placed him as king of carvers among his fellow craftsmen. His grandson, the broadcaster Douglas Kynoch, has brought to a wider audience the ignored talents of his remarkable grandfather.

Robert Warrack Morrison was born in 1890, and like many of his fellow north-east stone cutters, as a young man he worked in the granite yards of the USA, both before and after the First World War. But in 1918 a letter from his old firm, Morren and Co., Holland Street, Aberdeen, brought him back to Scotland for good. Throughout Britain, communities were anxious to erect war memorials to the war dead, and Morrison's skills were needed at home. His old boss, David Morren Senior, had recalled a granite wreath his young cutter had once effortlessly turned out in a lunch hour, confirming his belief that he had a craftsman of rare talent on his staff. Other skills included dispensing with the normal procedure of squaring off a block (a week per face, four weeks per block). Robert Morrison would just draw the square on both ends of the stone and knew instinctively the depth of stone to cut to, without the use of needles. He would carve the figure of a soldier in six weeks, as opposed to the usual six to nine months, with the results invariably being impressive.

The war memorial at Rhynie, Aberdeenshire, was probably Morrison's first, being unveiled on 30 May 1920. And indeed it appears that nearly all the Morren memorials may be credited to him, with the exception of Udny Station, which was carved by Frank Coutts. Examples of Morrison's work include the obelisk at Clatt and the Celtic crosses at Lumsden and Towie. He executed

Morrison was a carver of extraordinary speed and skill, apparently turning out a granite wreath in his lunch hour. His work is scattered all over the north-east of Scotland.

the sculpture of the soldiers at New Elgin and at Tarland, in which the vulnerable young soldier lad's face epitomises every mother's worst nightmare about the carnage of war. As Morrison's reputation grew commissions came from other parts of the country, and from England and Wales.

But the heyday of the memorial period effectively came to an end with the General Strike of 1926, and half the Morren yard's work became the building of prefabricated blocks, undertaken presumably to keep the yard going. For Robert Morrison, the regret that he must have felt at the curtailment of his creativity was compounded by the death of his wife, and his carving for her grave was a work which combined great skill and talent with personal grief. He died in 1945 at the age of fifty-five.

Trinity Cemetery, Aberdeen, lies between King Street and the sea, and can be approached from Errol Street. King Street can be found by following the central thoroughfare of Union Street to the east, where it becomes Castle Street. King Street goes off to the north eventually arriving at Bridge of Don. Less than halfway between Castle Street and Bridge of Don take either Errol Street or Urquhart Road to the right. The memorial gravestone is to be found by walking straight down from the main entrance of the cemetery for about 100 yards; the stone faces south on the right-hand side of the main path.

Photographic enterprise

The Fisher's Brae garage in the village of Coldingham had an unusual appendage, a gallery lined with photographs of the village and its surroundings, all dating between 1890 and 1912. The collection was not the product of a lifelong fascination of the garage owner, Bob Thomson, but the result of a lucky accident in 1983 which took him along to talk to Jimmy Brown, a retired market gardener.

Bob was helping his son Roy with a school project, and they were on the look-out for material such as old postcards of the village. Jimmy Brown had no old postcards, but he led Bob Thomson to his potting shed in which he had two boxes of sadly neglected half-plate glass negatives, thickly coated with decades of grime and dust. Jimmy explained that they were the work of John

Thrice-married (and once-eloped) Mrs Wood poses for her last husband, photographer John Wood, with the twins of their union.

John Wood caught the everyday events in his native Coldingham, and clearly had an eye for creating a photographic story. Little influence of Health and Safety issues here, or, indeed, concessions to modesty (note the striped bloomers in the left-hand window).

Dr Calder, local doctor at Coldingham owned a very splendid car in order to do his rounds, with a suitably dressed chauffeur to drive him around.

No record exists to determine if the couple clearly enjoying themselves here won a prize for their fancy-dress costumes.

Wood, who had come to live and work in Coldingham as a professional photographer in the 1880s.

After much research by Bob Thomson and his wife, Mary, they discovered that in 1890 Wood had married a widow called Margaret Kerr, who owned the general merchant's shop in the village High Street (now the premises of the Royal Bank of Scotland). John Wood had previously been married to a Glasgow girl, Rosina Lynch, in June 1877. At the time his occupation was listed as a joiner journeyman. Over the next thirteen years, Wood left the Glasgow area, arrived in Coldingham, divorced Rosina and married Margaret Kerr.

Margaret had already been married twice. Her first husband, Robert Kerr, died at the age of thirty-three; then, she fell in love with his brother, Thomas. As this would have been an illegal union, they eloped to France and were married in Boulogne in March 1882, but Thomas died six years later. Within eighteen months of his death she married John Wood.

Margaret had two sons and three daughters by her previous husband, and twins by John Wood. But she and Wood worked in the shop together until they sold it in 1895. John then went back to full-time photography, until he died at the age of sixty in 1914.

Some time after John Wood's death a village tradesman was asked to clean out his studio. This was done, but the tradesman used many of the photographic plates to glaze greenhouses and sheds, so that the majority of John's work was lost forever. Of the two boxes that were found, 600 plates were restored. The photographs date between 1890 and 1912 and were on display at Fisher's Brae. Now Bob Thomson has retired from the garage, the pictures are no longer on display in his gallery, but occasionally feature in local exhibitions. Behind each photograph is a family and human story, but perhaps the most extraordinary of all is the discovery of the photographic plates by Bob himself, and the very unusual marriage backgrounds of both John Wood and Margaret Kerr.

Coldingham, Berwickshire, is situated on the A1107, about ten miles north of Berwick-upon-Tweed.

Artistic licence

The Bell's Cherrybank Garden was the brainchild of Raymond Miquel, one-time supremo at Bell's Whisky in Perth before United Distillers took over the business. The garden was developed in the 1970s when the company's offices moved from Victoria Street in Perth to their present site on the outskirts of the town. Anxious to use the large area of surrounding land to advantage, Raymond Miquel wanted to enhance the area by creating something with a completely Scottish feel to be eventually used by Perth people. It had a host of natural advantages, such as a sloping and a flat area, a burn running along the foot of the small valley, and, not least, a jobbing gardener called Norrie Robertson, a very knowledgeable, hard-working and creative gardener.

A miniature golf course, in the form of a splendid pitch and putt, was created in the project's first phase, Scotland being the home of golf. Mr Miquel was proud of the high standards of the greens: 'We competed with Gleneagles for the calibre of the green and I think we were usually better!' Stage two of the project included the employment of a landscape architect to work on the

This enchanting statue by Iain MacKintosh of a girl washing her hair sits amid the Bell's Garden in Perth, which also houses the National Heather Collection.

remainder of the ground. It was during the planning stages for this second phase that the idea of pumping up water to make ponds amid the gardens was discussed. Mr Miquel thought that sculpture in the ponds elaborating themes of water and sea life would be very attractive. Artists came to see him with their sketchbooks of ideas, and, with his own background in art – he had attended art school and was about to study architecture before National Service – a selection of sculptures was chosen by him.

Each sculpture is the work of a modern Scottish artist. Lawrence Broderick is responsible for 'Mother and child' and 'Elation', and an otter, which when the surrounding water is quite still, forms a perfect reflected circle. Sadie McLellan created 'A Seed in Time', which revolves once every twenty-four seconds, as well as an Italian mosaic glass depicting the Bell's coat of arms, 'Nunc et semper' ('Now and always'). An Ian Hamilton Finlay sundial in the shape of an eye is here too, and an enchanting Iain MacKintosh figure of a girl washing her hair.

Some of the original features of the garden, such as the pitch and putt, have been buried under the encroachment of a car park and extension to the offices. However, the garden is now renowned for the National Heather Collection, which means that any known heather which a heather enthusiast wants to see should be housed here. The first batch of 100 varieties of heather were planted in 1988, followed by regular planting every year. Bell's see the final collection encompassing around 1,000 different species.

'Anyone can apply to start a national collection of plants,' explained Norrie, 'for instance there is someone down south who holds the collection of rhubarb!' The role of national collections is to conserve, investigate and display the diversity of our gardening heritage, and this collection comes under the guidance of the Northern Horticultural Society. 'Bell's decided that they would like to have the national collection of heather, which consists of ling or true heather, *Calluna*, the heaths, *Erica*, and the *Daboecia* – it doesn't have to be the complete collection though, but you have to aim to have three plants of each variety.'

It all sounded a wonderful idea, a Scottish company holding the largest collection, and a national one to boot. And it also sounds quite an easy idea to implement – organise a series of orders from the Scottish heather growers and plant them up. Well, not quite. The heathers come, in fact, from all over Britain. Each region in the UK has its own variety of heather, each one different. From all over Europe there are yet more species, but Bell's have not bought any from outside the UK, as Norrie explained that there is rather a nasty plant disease the foreign varieties could bring in. Anyway, they have not yet exhausted the varieties available in this country.

They also have to be careful of the 'sports', or freak, one-off plants, as well as the very closely related varieties, and the Heather Society keeps a sharp eye open for these.

When the new heather garden idea was first mooted, the soil in the area, uncultivated for forty years, was found to be quite unsuitable as a home for heather, which hates the lime content found strongly in the soil. The lime came from rocks used as the base for the new western bypass round Perth, less than 500 metres away. These rocks raised the height of the road thirty metres, and the lime had seeped down the hill and saturated the ground intended for the heather garden. Norrie Robertson, the head gardener, was not one to be put off by such a trifle: 'The solution was to raise the heather beds above the water table. Lime seeps downwards, so provided the heather roots do not touch this water, all is well.'

The beds, which now sweep in curves round the hill, are all little hummocks of peat-based lime-free soil, and the heathers thrive.

To find Bell's Cherrybank Garden, leave the A9 Stirling to Perth road at Broxden roundabout and follow signs to Perth.

A secret room in Peebles

Were it not for the fact that the Alexander frieze in the Chambers Institute in Peebles was and is attached to the walls of the room, it might well have gone the way of all the other sculptures which filled the room – ousted and lost forever.

The Museum Room at the Institute originally housed a collection of plaster casts, copies of some of the world's most famous pieces of sculpture, such as the Apollo Belvedere, the

Only chance, and the fact that they were firmly fixed to the walls, saved these plaster casts from being destroyed. They comprise much of the most significant section of the Elgin Marbles, and are within the Secret Room in the Chambers Institute in Peebles.

Venus de Milo and the Dying Gladiator. The room was closed to the public in the late 1950s and used as a library store. Much of the free-standing plasterwork which it had contained was destroyed, with only the wall-mounted plaster friezes remaining.

These friezes consist of a 62-foot section of the most significant portions of the Elgin Marbles and a complete facsimile of the Triumph of Alexander by the Danish sculptor Bertil Thorvaldsen. This latter frieze is extremely rare in Britain and it is usually only sections of this work which are exhibited. As far as can be ascertained, the only other complete version in Britain has been restored and displayed at the Harris Museum in Preston. The original frieze was executed by Thorvaldsen in 1812 (taking only three months to complete) for the Palazzo Quirinale, which was then being decorated for the expected arrival of Napoleon in Rome. Marble copies were made later for the Villa Carlotta, Lake Como, and the Christiansborg Palace, Copenhagen.

The frieze was an allegory, Napoleon's entry into Rome being compared with that of Alexander the Great into Babylon in 331 BC after his defeat of the Persian King Darius. History relates that Alexander marched on Babylon expecting to lay siege to it and was surprised to see the citizens coming out to meet him bearing gifts and welcoming him into their city. The frieze therefore shows the procession of Babylonians while Alexander's army rides forward to enter the city.

Thorvaldsen was born in Copenhagen in 1770 and despite the poverty of his childhood, gained admission to the Royal Academy of Fine Arts in Copenhagen, where he won the gold medal for sculpture, entitling him to the Academy's travelling scholarship. In 1797 he arrived in Rome, at that time considered the artistic capital of the world. In time he established himself as one of the leading sculptors of his day. During the forty years he spent in Rome, Thorvaldsen received commissions for sculptures which are now to be found all over Europe.

He returned to Denmark in 1838 to a hero's welcome and spent his last years creating a museum in Copenhagen for his works and his collection. He died in 1844 and was given a state funeral. He was buried in a tomb in the courtyard of his museum.

Dr William Chambers, born in Peebles in 1800, became a publisher and his company flourishes to this day and still bears his name. He probably commissioned the friezes specially for the museum, and the section of the Parthenon frieze was deliberately chosen to complement Thorvaldsen's work.

Relief sculpture, especially narrative friezes, was one of the important neo-classical developments around 1800. Most neo-classical works at that time made reference to Roman examples, such as Trajan's Column. Thorvaldsen's importance lies in his understanding of Greek sculpture which was only just beginning to be appreciated in its own right. The Alexander frieze contains many compositional elements and motifs from the Parthenon frieze drawings which were circulating in Rome in his time. Hence the relevance of the juxtaposition of the two friezes in the Museum Room, sometimes also called the Secret Room because it was so long forgotten.

The exact origin of the casts of the Parthenon frieze is not recorded. Their purpose would have been both to educate and assist in the study of art, since drawing from classical antiquity was an essential part of artistic training in the nineteenth century. Most of the large museums in Britain acquired casts of the Elgin Marbles. It is probable that those in the Chambers Institute were taken from other casts which had undergone some restoration, as heads of several figures are nineteenth-century additions.

The Secret Room is found within the Tweeddale Museum, Chambers Institute, in the High Street in Peebles. Peebles is on the A703 about twenty miles south of Edinburgh.

Robert Thompson, the 'mouse carver'

The Isle of Ensay is about as far west as this particular mouse ventured, and it has stayed put for a century. On the island of Canna another has been lurking, and in 2005 was happily saved from rats, being placed in safe hiding until the danger was over. Puzzled?

A multitude of carved mice exist across many Church of Scotland churches, from Troon to Dornoch, Skye to Moffat, and at King's College Chapel in Aberdeen to St Peter's, the aptly named Episcopal Church in Peterhead. But the carver came from Kilburn, a small Yorkshire village where he has belatedly become something of a celebrity, and even spawned a dynasty. Born there in 1876, Robert Thompson was the son of the local joiner and wheelwright, but was first apprenticed not to the gentle work of a woodcarver but to what he considered to be the harsher craft of engineer. He hated it, and finally after five miserable years returned to the world of joinery with his father.

Much happier, he continued his apprenticeship and might well have followed his father as a jobbing carpenter, but on a visit to Ripon Cathedral his vocation pivoted to more intricate wood carving. He fell in love with the rippling surface which a little-known fifteenth-century carver called William Bomflet had achieved on oak, achieved with the use of an ancient tool called an adze. Thompson was enchanted and raised his expertise and skill to the extent that his first commission, from the monks of Ampleforth College, was followed by York Minster and then the free-standing altar sticks at Westminster Abbey. These bear his signature, a tiny, expressive mouse carved into a hidden crevice on each commission. The story of why he adopted this humble addition to his work and became an expert carver of mice, which served as his signature within places of worship far and wide, was a tale told to his grandson:

> I was carving a beam on a church roof when another carver, Charlie Barker, murmured something about being as poor as church mice, and on the spur of the moment I carved one. Afterwards I decided to adopt the mouse as a trademark, because I thought how a mouse manages to scrape and chew away the hardest of wood with its chisel-like teeth and works quietly, with nobody taking much notice. I thought that maybe like the workshop hidden away in the Hambleton Hills, it is what you might call industry in a quiet place, so I included a mouse on all my work.

Thompson's mice can now be seen everywhere from York Minster to Troon, Moffat, Dornoch, Skye, the Isle of Ensay and King's College Chapel in Aberdeen – but only if you know where to look.

In the Aberdeenshire town of Peterhead, within St Peter's Episcopal Church, there is a mouse lurking behind the altar, on a small shelf to the right-hand side. However, the mouse on the island of Canna is not at home. This one is in hiding from the rats which have overrun the island and which were endangering the very fabric of the small church there, including the Thompson carved mouse. When the rats are safely away the Thompson mouse will return to his rightful place on Canna.

In the meantime, another Thompson mouse is resident on another island, that of Ensay, off the coast of Harris. Tony Scherr, the present-day guardian and recorder of its history, writes of Ensay Church that, together with the island, it had long belonged to the Macleods of Dunvegan. In 1834 the Macleods sold Ensay to the Earl of Dunmore and in 1856 Dunmore sold the island to Archibald Stewart, 'a tacksman of Dunvegan'. A descendant of Archibald Stewart, Mrs Jessie Scott, was an Episcopalian and in

Although the remote Ensay Church was built earlier than 1549, the door, carved by Robert Thompson, the celebrated woodcarver of Kilburn, Yorkshire, was carried over in a boat less than 50 years ago, and can still be seen, as can the distinctive Thompson mouse trademark.

1909 she set about restoring the old chapel which was only a stone's throw from the big house.

Mrs Scott, when on the island, lived at Ensay House, and according to old Gaelic papers, 'She was handsome in bearing and appearance. She was slender, tall, stern and forbidding, she was of good character, pleasing manners and clung to the straight and narrow path.' Johnny Stewart, the bard, who was a shepherd on Pabbay, saw Ensay House and sang its praises: 'Brass and silver pipes draw water from the rock, skill without blemish guarantees that it will endure.'

With zeal, Jessie Scott set about restoring the church to its original and sacred purpose. She cleaned it out and with simple taste and dignity she fitted it once more as a place of worship. Save for some pointing, the walls were left in their rough and rude state. The roof was completely re-slated. A heavy oak door and cemented floor were added. The altar, altar rail, reredos and lectern were made in mahogany. Above the door she placed a stone bearing the following legend, *Chaid an eaglais so air ath-thogail, sa bleadhna 1910 chun gloir Dhe agus mar chuimneachan air Naomh Chiluim Colle agus na mhanaich a thug a'soisgeul do na h-eileanan agus thog an eaglais so air tus*, which, translated into English, is 'This church was rebuilt in 1910 to the glory of God and as a memorial to Saint Columba and the monks who brought the Gospel to these islands and built the church in the beginning.'

At the time of these alterations, the island was in the large and scattered parish of the rector of Portree on the Isle of Skye.

In 1931 Jessie Scott died and in her will she made over to the Scottish Episcopal Bishop of Argyll and the Isles the 'old Church at Ensay, restored by her, with the grounds enclosed and all furniture, vestments and plate belonging to the Church – together with a sum of £200 (Less Estate and Legacy duty). Net received – £179, for the general upkeep of the Church'. She also laid down some conditions, which included the proviso that the church had to be used twice a year for services.

However, the period from 1935 to the mid-1950s was a barren period for Ensay. The church once again fell into disrepair. It was then that John David came onto the scene. John had known and loved Ensay for many years and when the opportunity came for him to buy Ensay House, he quickly grasped it. Son of the late Bishop David of Liverpool, who had also been headmaster at Rugby, John David was a medical specialist who practised in Ghana and it was on his all too infrequent leaves from there that he worked on his beloved house and church. He restored all that Jessie Scott had done and also added a distinctive new oaken door, and it was a door carved by Robert Thompson. Quite how he managed to acquire this door, or indeed transport it over to the island, is unknown.

In 1975, Penny Downie of Strond in Harris was married in Ensay Church to Carey Coombs. Eighteen years later, in March 1993, Douglas Cameron, Bishop of Argyll and the Isles, was to ordain Penny's father, James Downie, as priest-in-charge of Christ Church, Harris. He continued, often accompanied by Bishop Douglas Cameron, to take services on Ensay until his death in 2004.

In 1979, with his retirement in sight, John David died suddenly and tragically in Ghana. He had looked forward so much to retiring to Ensay where he could continue his work on Ensay House and his honorary custodianship of Ensay Church. He must have had a premonition about his death, for the previous year he had shown the builder where, at the side of the church, he would like his ashes to be buried. His family were later to put a stone over the spot, on which was simply written: 'John David – he loved this place'. In his will, he left Ensay House to his nephews and nieces, who continue to play their part in the life of Ensay Church. He also left a bequest of money to St Peter's Church in Stornoway which was later used for repairs on Ensay Church.

On 6 September 1986 one of John David's nieces, Virginia David, married David Murray in Ensay Church. In June of each year, weather permitting, an annual pilgrimage to Ensay is made by the Harris congregation and their friends, and it remains a very special place to all who worship there.

The island of Ensay is just to the west of Harris and is privately owned. The legacy and work of Robert Thompson continues within his home village of Kilburn in Yorkshire where oak furniture is constructed.

Of foolhardy marquises, foolish titles and happy dragons

Taymouth Castle is undergoing restoration, taking this most extravagant of extravaganzas, an exemplar of wealth unwisely spent, from semi-dereliction and decadence back to supreme comfort. However, the twenty-first-century reconstruction will also retain some of the castle's secrets, which will one day be available for all to see – at a cost, for this will be a luxury hotel in the same mould as it was a luxury castle for one family.

The Breadalbanes of Taymouth appeared, in the early nineteenth century, impregnable. They could have walked across from their castle at Kenmore, on the banks of the Tay, to the west coast of Scotland without leaving their own land.

The original castle, the ancient Castle Balloch, complete by 1559, was typical of its time as it was constructed on the Z-plan – a fortified house with a hall and chamber. Its owner, Sir Colin Campbell of Glenorchy, died in 1583 and his title passed to Black Duncan Campbell of the Cowl who was a pioneer of forestation and planted a lot of the imposing trees still alive at Taymouth.

Black Duncan's great-grandson John became the first Earl of Breadalbane, and his son, the second earl, commissioned William Adam to completely remodel the old castle. By 1733 a classical mansion house with two flanking pavilions linked to the main block by quadrant wings had been completed and Sir John renamed the building Taymouth Castle.

In 1782 the title and estates passed to a distant cousin, John Campbell of Carwhin, who became the fourth earl. He had secured a fortune when he married his wife and it was this money that enabled him to make the most significant changes to the castle under the direction of Archibald and James Elliot in 1805. Most of the old castle was demolished leaving only the Adam wings. A new central tower, built in grey-green stone locally quarried and rising eighty feet, was completed in 1809 and stands unaltered today. The Grand Tower has stained-glass windows in the very top – a remarkable feat when you consider it was built before scaffolding and would have been completed using ropes and pulleys. In 1831 the earl was created first Marquis of Breadalbane.

The second marquis adapted the west wing between 1838 and 1842 to include a library and state bedrooms which were used by Queen Victoria and the Prince Consort in 1842. These works were carried out under James Gillespie Graham who completely encased the old east wing and linked it to the main building with a tall Gothic room originally intended as a chapel but which subsequently became the Banner Hall, leading into the library. And it is in this library that the first of the many Taymouth touches of cheek is revealed.

Three-quarters of the way down the room, amid the many library shelves, which were filled with leather-bound tomes, is a secret door leading into a passageway and then directly into the royal bedroom. The books on this secret door appear perfectly genuine to the straying eye, this eye more than likely being glazed by the sheer volume of books, ornamental wooden fretwork, intricate ceiling, screens which neatly fold back, like elaborate shutters to let in more light, and the views from the rooms themselves. The titles of the books, though, give the game away. At eye level, right by the crack where the bookshelves end and the door can open, is a leather-bound spine with the embossed title *Inigo on Secret Entrances*, above *Campaign in the British Army by one of the German Leg, Chronological Account of the Date Tree*, and, rather aptly, considering some of the family's future conduct, *Shype of Fools*.

If one could have glanced into the royal bedroom the bed would have filled much of the room, being massive in size and, rumour had it, dressed and draped in fabric which glistened with silver, resulting from the genuine precious metal being flattened to tissue slenderness and woven into the fabric. This is was but one of the sets of rooms prepared for the royal personages. The marquis had taken the precaution of preparing two suites, on different sides of the castle.

Twenty years after the visit of Queen Victoria and Prince Albert, in 1862, the second marquis died and was succeeded by his distant cousin John Alexander Gavin Campbell. Gavin and his wife, Alma, were both gamblers and ran up debts equal to the value of the entire estate. Alma was restricted by her husband to the boundaries of the castle estate, in a desperate attempt to prevent her gambling, but she simply managed to bring in her gambling cronies in order to continue – and one small, circular room at the front of the castle has a set of mirrors on the ceiling arranged like a fan, one of which is of sufficient magnifying strength to reveal the hand of cards below, hence providing one of the card players (Alma supposedly?) with an advantage.

Local tongues tell of the marquis visiting his local bank in nearby Aberfeldy to be told that he had no money or credit remaining. In a rage he returned to the castle, with murder in his heart, but rather than turning the gun on his wife, he supposedly shot all his horses except for one white one, and it was in a carriage pulled by that horse that the marquis and marchioness left the castle forever, so fulfilling a prophesy by the Lady of Lawers that the family would leave with one single white steed. They were the last Breadalbanes to live at Taymouth. The earl sold off part of the estate in December 1920, and then in 1922 the estates and contents of the castle were sold at lots by public auction to meet the earl's debts.

There was no single owner found for the castle. Instead it was sold to a consortium of businessmen based in Glasgow who set up the Taymouth Castle Hotel Company.

The Taymouth Castle Hotel Company developed the castle into a first-class hotel at a cost of nearly £100,000. It had electric light and an electric elevator and James Braid laid out the park as a golf course. The Taymouth Castle Hydro-Hotel opened in June 1923 but the company went into liquidation on 29 March 1926. The next day the castle and estate were bought by the Taymouth Castle Hotel Company Ltd. and operated as a hotel until 1939.

At the outbreak of war in 1939, the castle was requisitioned as a hospital for Polish servicemen until the end of the war. In 1950, it was leased to the government and was operated as a Civil Defence College until the late 1960s. It was in 1969, when it became a private school for the children of American servicemen stationed in Europe, that the castle was last occupied. The school was closed in 1975 and since then the building has lain empty. But within this fairytale exterior still lie many secrets of the various builders and owners, waiting to be seen. One final laugh can be found in the painted ceiling of the extensively decorated Chinese Room. Amid a frieze of dragons, one creature looks particularly happy. It is a very female dragon, endowed with substantial bosoms, amid dozens of male dragons. No wonder she looks smug.

Taymouth Castle lies just to the east of Kenmore in Perthshire. It is possible to park in the square in Kenmore and walk along by the River Tay, viewing the castle from a short distance away.

5

Tales of travel by sail, train or royal command

The ship's figurehead

The 'Widden Wife', or the 'White Lady' to use her grander title, stands proud today, restored, re-painted and replaced in her former position, almost exactly sixty-five years after her first arrival on the shores of Shetland, at East Yell.

The sad thing about her arrival was that she did not intend to land at all. She is the figurehead from the Gothenburg-registered, three-masted 1487-ton barque *Bohus*, which was wrecked on the Ness of Queyon, East Yell, on the afternoon of Saturday 26 April 1924. The tale of her sinking is contained in the Shetland Sub Aqua Club's account of Shetland shipwrecks, of which there are, tragically, very many.

The refurbished figurehead which now stands as a memorial on the site was for a long time in a bad state of repair, despite being loyally maintained by members of the local community. The task of restoration was painstakingly carried out by the Shetland Amenity Trust, who point out that as far as they know this is the only example of such a figurehead being restored and replaced on the site of a shipwreck. A replica of the original is on display at the Old Haa at Burravoe.

Built of iron in 1892 by the Grangemouth Dockyard Company at Alloa, the *Bohus* was owned by Donetz, Witt and Company, Hamburg. Apart from her commercial use, she was a training ship for officers of the German Navy and mercantile marine. Aboard at the time of the sinking were sixteen crew, twenty-two cadets and a stowaway.

For two weeks prior to her sinking, weather conditions had been extremely severe and a number of wrecks had occurred round the Shetland coast. *A Shetland Parish Doctor*, by Dr H. Taylor, gives the basic account of the sinking of the *Bohus*.

Although built by the Grangemouth Dockyard Company in Alloa in 1892, the *Bohus* was owned by a German company when she went down in 1924 with the loss of four lives. The figurehead was washed ashore and stands as a memorial to those lost at East Yell on Shetland.

The master of the ship, Captain Blume, said that they had experienced very bad weather since leaving Gothenburg, Sweden, on 25 April bound for Taltal, Chile, carrying 250 tons of sand ballast. None of the officers had set eyes on sun or stars, so the vessel was being steered by 'guess and God'. Unknown to Captain Blume, the vessel was 60 miles off course on reaching Shetland. About noon on Saturday 26 April, Captain Blume caught sight of land which he considered to be Fair Isle, but which was actually Out Skerries. A north-west course was set in the belief that this would enable the vessel to pass between Fair Isle and Sumburgh Head, taking them into open sea. A south-easterly gale was blowing with a heavy sea and haze. Land was impossible to see a mile from shore.

Early in the afternoon, land was reported on the port and starboard bows. The captain realised his ship was coming in on a dangerous coast about which he knew next to nothing. He tried to get the *Bohus* to come round but was unable to do so. One of the anchors was dropped but the cable broke after about 25 fathoms had been run out. The vessel at this point was close to the coast.

Eyewitness Hughie Thompson takes up the story:

> The visibility was not good. That was partly the reason why she came in on a lee shore. She wasn't able to see anything you might say to windward, so she just gradually drifted doon . . . weal, I wid say driftin', because she wasn't sailing. She didn't have enough sails on her to sail off 'o the shore. But, that wis the position. She just gradually drove on the shore. But there was only me Fauder, an' Fauder-in-law an' me. That wis the only three men that wis there when she did come ashore.

The captain attempted to bring the vessel onto the other tack by bringing the wind round the stern, but the *Bohus* ran broadside onto the Ness of Queyon with her bow pointing eastward.

Hughie continued:

> . . . it wis only a short distance from the shore, but it was fairly deep water, you see. There were no rocks or anything for them to get on between the ship and the shore. Just open water you may say from where they stranded until they cam ashore.

When the vessel grounded, several of the crew leapt overboard, making their way to the shore. Shortly after running onto the rocks, the vessel fell to seaward. Those on board slid into the water

> . . . it wis rather a sad sight to see them all in the water at one time, an' us trying to held what we would, you see. But, there was only four lost out of a crew . . . I mean, the whole lot on board, there was about forty, so it was . . . I considered that they had a marvellous escape, that there wasn't more lost, because a considerable amount o' sea was running on the shore at that time.

One of the four dead, Gustav Droger, the ship's cook, actually reached land, only to 'take to the hills', never to be seen alive again. It is supposed that he must have fallen over the cliffs. Two men are buried in Mid Yell graveyard.

Only twenty minutes or so after *Bohus* struck the coast, she split near the bows and went down. It was some time later that the figurehead drifted ashore, to be eventually erected on the shore in memory of those who had died.

Yell is a large island to the north of mainland Shetland. The figurehead at Queyon is well signposted.

A Tahitian princess at Anstruther

Tetuanui i reia i te Raiatea was a Tahitian princess of Haapiti who was married in 1856 at the tender age of fourteen to John Brander from Elgin. John Brander had many business interests in the Pacific, and was described by the American Henry Adams as trading 'coconuts by the million: his culture of pearls produced pearl-shell for Europe by the ton; his ships transported all the trade of the islands; his revenue was vast and his wealth estimated in thousands'.

Into this wealthy world the new Mrs Brander walked with confidence and charm. Her parties were legion and in her capacity as first lady of Tahiti, she entertained the Duke of Edinburgh in 1868, having visited Elgin with her husband in 1865.

John Brander died in 1877 and the following year Tetuanui i reia i te Raiatea married her manager, George Dairsie, who hailed from a family which had produced generations of Anstruther town councillors, bailies, ship-masters, fish-curers, tanners and shoemakers. After adding three more children, Georgina, George and Lieumonte, to the nine she had had with John Brander, the couple sailed for Anstruther and retirement in 1892 and settled in the fine family house of Johnston Lodge.

Tetuanui i reia i te Raiatea died in 1898 at the age of fifty-five and is buried with her husband in the parish churchyard of

Gravestone of the Tahitian Princess, Tetuanui i reia i te Raiatea, in Anstruther. She successively married two successful Scots businessmen, bearing twelve children, and gained a reputation as an eminent hostess, even entertaining the then Duke of Edinburgh in 1868.

Anstruther. R. B. Cunninghame Graham's short story 'A Princess' was inspired by her life.

Anstruther, Fife, is nine miles south of St Andrews on the B9131 or fourteen miles on the A917. The gravestone is placed on the wall of the parish church.

Queen Guinevere

The road to Barry Hill, with its right-angled bends, lack of traffic and gently climbing gradient to the glens, creates a feeling of mysticism and shadowy adventure that adds some credence to its reputed connection with Arthurian legend. Drive up there on a misty, dank day and it might even send a shiver down your spine. Perhaps that is because you could be following in the fleeing footsteps of Queen Guinevere.

The story of the Round Table is widely believed to be rooted in south-west England, where in Somerset the story of Arthur and his knights has been made into a mini industry. Even more intense speculation and tourist potential hovers over the Cornish coast at Tintagel.

All this is in spite of historian Archie McKerracher's carefully researched article in the August 1989 issue of the *Scots Magazine* which places the Round Table (or tabloid rotunda as he describes it) at Stenhousemuir.

The legend climaxes with Sir Lancelot, one of Arthur's knights, having a love affair with Queen Guinevere. This was bound to end in tears, and indeed things went rapidly downhill, culminating in Guinevere's death. This ancient tale, redolent of chivalry and honour, also contains a heady mixture of passion, treason, betrayals, duels and grisly death.

It is the death of Queen Guinevere that links the tale with Meigle in Perthshire. Granted, it is a long way from Cornwall to Meigle, but truth in this case is as twisted as King Arthur's chain mail.

The story was popularised by a Welsh bishop, Geoffrey of Monmouth, in his *History of the Kings of Britain*, published in 1136. The problem is that although exotic remains of fifth- and sixth-century pottery originally from the eastern Mediterranean have been uncovered at Tintagel, the romantic castle itself, tottering on a cliff, was not constructed until the end of the twelfth century, six centuries after Guinevere was reputed to have lived there.

Reputed is the key word here. The whole Arthurian saga, exploited and embellished by writers and by Hollywood over the centuries, has never been proved to the based on hard fact.

An American professor, Norma Goodrich, though, is firmly convinced that Guinevere did exist, and she claims that after twenty years searching for proof, she found it at Meigle in 1991. She reveals that it has always been claimed in medieval manuscripts that the real version of the death of the queen was written on stones, and within the museum at Meigle, she reckons she has found them.

The slab which she says tells the full tale stands theatrically in the centre of the museum, an intriguing example of the stunning skills of Pictish stonemasons. Skilfully carved on both sides of this immense slab are figures of a horseman, his followers, hunting dogs and an angel peeping out from the top corner. While the horsemen march confidently on, below them stands a long tunic-clad figure with arms outstretched, as though calmly awaiting fate. Possibly a dire fate, as the figure is flanked by four lions or mastiff-like creatures, obviously slavering to catch their quarry.

Now, the plot thickens. While some authorities on Celtic and Pictish stones claim such scenes to be biblical, Daniel in the lions' den in this case, Professor Goodrich begs to differ. She points to the hinge-like pieces of stones projecting on either side. These, she claims, confirm the true existence of a story alluded to by medieval scholars. It was a reference, carved during the sixteenth century, to a triptych in which three slabs of stones were linked by mortice and tenon joints.

Such a stone as the one at Meigle was certainly a very special memorial, to a VIP at least, even a royal personage. It might well have been part of a hinged group of three.

Historic Scotland write, in their official guide to the Meigle Museum, which is sited in the old schoolhouse next door to the central village church:

> Meigle must have been an important centre of the church both in the Pictish period, and after the union of the Pictish and Scottish Kingdoms around AD 840. The clearest evidence for this is the survival of these superb carved stones. But in addition we had evidence of a scribe called Thana here, around 840, who is said to have written about in the early history of St Andrew.

A 'green shadowy mound' in the churchyard at Meigle is said to mark the queen's grave, the spot at which the stones originally lay. Local folklore warns against any young girl walking over the grave for by this she risks being rendered infertile. The mound itself has never been excavated.

The mound in Meigle churchyard is supposedly the grave of Queen Guinevere. It was originally surrounded by elaborate Pictish stones, which are now housed in the nearby museum.

So why was Queen Guinevere apparently buried here?

Some experts hold fast to the theory that King Arthur was in fact a warrior leader, whose battling calibre elevated him, if only in times of crisis, to kingship. He left Queen Guinevere in order to make a pilgrimage to Rome, and while he was away the queen and his nephew, Mordred, whom Arthur had named as regent in his absence, became lovers, and eventually took over as rulers. Upon hearing of this, Arthur challenged Mordred in battle, and although he slew his rival, was fatally wounded himself. Some versions of the tale now credit Guinevere with retiring to a convent to finish her days as a nun, but the Scots version has a far less charitable conclusion.

Such was the dishonour now enveloping Guinevere, who had betrayed her husband and also plotted treason, that a death as macabre as possible was planned. She was held at the iron-age fort of Barry Hill, or Dun Barve, and of the many endings to this story two versions predominate.

One is that some time later she fled but was hunted and set upon by a pack of wolfhounds, dying from the injuries they inflicted.

Another version describes how Arthur was still very much alive and, having dispatched Mordred, was so enraged by Guinevere's infidelity that he caused her to be torn to pieces by wild animals.

So instead of the stone carving representing Daniel in the lions' den, it shows Guinevere being torn apart by dogs or other animals. In any event, she was given the belated honour of a burial in sacred ground, the spot being marked by a stone depicting her bloody demise.

Doubts have always been cast on whether the Picts ever possessed a written language, communicating instead by symbols or a type of hieroglyphics. Possibly they used Latin, but story-telling via carving was an essential part of their culture.

The Statistical Account of 1791 elaborates on the whole story of the queen at Meigle. She was also known as Vanora, Vanera, Wanor, and Helena, and the account remarks that 'the whole history is involved in fables'.

This story is still perpetuated in the 1979 Statistical Account, which describes how the Meigle Women's Rural Institute in 1926 designed and embroidered a banner depicting the queen as shown on one of the stones, wherein she is carved in the guise of an angel, close to the figure of King Arthur riding on horseback.

Another supposed relic of the days of King Arthur existed at one time on the estate of – not surprisingly – Arthurstone. A large stone, called Arthur's stone, from which the estate had indeed taken its name, stood there until 1791, when it was used in the building of the farm at Arthurbank, close to the large mansion house of Arthurstone.

What still exists and relates to the fable are the carved Meigle Pictish stones, Arthurstone as a name, and Barry Hill with the remains of the fort. This huge fort stood in a commanding position crowning the area, with ramparts and ditches marked clearly on archaeological maps, as well as a smattering of smaller outer forts, and a weem or underground dwelling. With positive proof never likely to emerge, the choice of which (if any) story to believe is up to the reader.

Meigle, Perthshire, with its churchyard adjacent to the kirk in the centre of the village, is on the junction of the B954 and the A94 about sixteen miles north-west of Dundee.

Barry Hill is to the east of the B954, a couple of miles north of Alyth. OS map reference NO263505.

Empress of Morocco

Only one Scots lassie appears to have been an Arab empress. Given the ways in which she attained this rank, the tale could be open to conjecture, but a rollicking good story it is.

The future empress, Helen Gloag, was born around the early part of the eighteenth century. For a future royal lady, her birthplace was humble – she was born in a cottage which stood at the Mill of Steps, which lies between Muthill and Braco, in Perthshire.

As in all the best romantic tales, Helen Gloag was alleged to have been beautiful, red-headed, statuesque and 'possessed of clarity of speech and manner well above her station of life at that time'. So it is not surprising that the next we hear of Helen is that she had grown up, fallen out with her parents and left home 'taking with her nothing but what she had on'.

She next came to light crossing the Atlantic for a new life in America, but the vessel was captured by an African pirate and the crew and passengers were sold as slaves. But Helen was clearly a lady of vision. She is next heard of as 'captivating the affections of the Emperor', which goes to prove the effects of red hair. He married her, and by her had two sons. Apparently she never again left Morocco, but continued to write to her parents.

An account of her life, first published about 1780, tried to authenticate her story. It was pointed out that at that time Helen's cousin was a Duncan MacGregor, well known in the area as a survivor of the '45 Jacobite uprising. He boasted that he had a cousin who was an empress. Moreover, Helen's brother had been a sea captain, and when he died in the Mill of Steps cottage, he left behind articles, such as china, which had originated in

Morocco. These mementoes of Helen then went to John Bayne, a farmer at Lurg.

Far-fetched the whole story could be, but more evidence emerged. John Shearer's *Antiquities of Strathearn* quoted a tale of a projected expedition to Morocco by the British government which came to nothing. Apparently, Helen's two sons, the Moroccan princes, had appealed to the British government for assistance. Pointing out that their mother had been British, they requested help in toppling pretenders to the throne of Morocco which should have rightfully been theirs on the death of their father, the Emperor. The British actually went as far as fitting out an expedition in Gibraltar until the news came that the two young princes, grandsons of the elderly couple at Steps, had been killed.

Mill of Steps, Perthshire, is less than a mile from the centre of Muthill. Muthill is three miles south of Crieff. From Muthill take the secondary, unmarked southbound road which is the old straight military road and connects up again with the A822 south to Dunblane. Mill of Steps is on the Machany Water.

Off the rails – literally

Strathdon and the surrounding glens of Aberdeenshire are far from the main railway lines. Most were never even remotely likely to obtain their own branch railway so it is all the more confusing to find here the greatest sprinkling anywhere in the country of old railway carriages, settled down comfortably on the farms.

Each farm looks as though it has had a share-out of the spoils of Dr Beeching (the former chairman of the British Railways board who axed most of the branch railways in the 1960s, and whose name is synonymous with the disappearance of a whole way of life). Nowadays, more than thirty years on from the demise of the rural railway network in Scotland, these carriages sit like elderly whales, beached far from their natural habitat, sinking comfortably and with dignity into the landscape. For all the world it appears as though a locomotive has cast off its carriages piecemeal around the farms.

As a curious child in the 1950s, I can remember being puzzled by the sight of just such a railway carriage, its tattered blinds with their silk tassels flapping through an open window, happily home to an assortment of hens and a cockerel at one end, while at the other, a pig poked its snout through a type of outsize rough-hewn cat flap. How did such a large, unwieldy contraption manoeuvre its way to an area which has never had a railway line?

The key to the solution is the former Great North of Scotland Railway Works, for it was a happy and profitable marriage between railway employee enterprise and the crafty Aberdonian farmer.

'When I worked in Glasgow, prior to coming up here to Inverurie in 1963, we just burned them,' explained the late Jimmy Brown, who had had the job of selling the old vehicles. 'In Glasgow it wasn't worth breaking them up for scrap. But at Inverurie Loco Works there was a dozen or so old vans and carriages leaving the works each week. Two contractors took them out – Messrs Reid of Insch and Bruce of Inverurie – and it was astonishing how they could place these unwieldy vehicles anywhere they were wanted using only a couple of empty old drums and some sleepers.'

Jimmy Brown remembered how farmers and their families found their way to the works, and of course they had to inspect each and every vehicle before they made their minds up. The scrap vehicles were scattered all around the works, so this proved a time-consuming exercise until Jimmy arranged for them to be lined up in front of the works office and restricted each customer's choice to the first three vehicles in the queue.

Jimmy's predecessor had warned him to get the money before anything left the works and the only time he gave a farmer credit – because he was taking a quantity – he had to threaten to take the vans back before they were finally paid for. The farmers all had cheque books and it amazed him the way they would throw their blank cheque books down before the typist to fill in the details. Another thing that puzzled him was the way the farmers usually only turned up at the works when it was raining – until some kind local soul pointed out to the townie that, clearly, they could not work on their farms when it was raining.

Far distant from any railway line, the Strathdon area, Aberdeenshire, is dotted with many ancient railway carriages, which were sold to farmers in the '50s to house extra farm workers, hens, seed, animal feed, and any other farming flotsam.

Railway carriages in Upper Donside, Aberdeenshire, still contain fluttering ragged blinds at the windows, and are evocative reminders of landscapes visited by trains before Beeching axed many of the more remote lines.

The price of the vehicles was £1.25 per linear foot (30 cm), which worked out at £22.75 for the average covered goods van. But some vans were in better condition than others and Jimmy became concerned when he was left with a line of vans with holes in their roofs or broken doors: the shrewd north-east farmers did not want these. But Jimmy was a match for the farmers and just as cunning. He plumped up the price of the decent vehicles to £30 and slashed a few pounds off the price of a broken one, so the latter sold like hot cakes.

The condemned vans were lined up for sale, and the wheels and attendant metalwork, which were not included in the sale, were taken off by oxyacetylene burner. Then the carriages were loaded onto the trailer for the final journey. Tales of Jimmy's commercial success reached the ears of the British Rail headquarters down in Derby who sent someone up to investigate how he was making so much money out of old vans. Alas, by this stage, in the late 1970s, the supply was running out, and any plans to create a thriving new business in Inverurie, no matter how impressive his sales figures appeared, hit the buffers.

So vital was the extra space provided by a train carriage on these remote farms that the Aden Country Park, Aberdeenshire, acquired one in 1991 as an essential component part of the typical Buchan farm of the 1950s when they created their Heritage Centre. The smallholding of Hareshowe of Ironside had been owned by Miss Margaret Barron who had lived there since 1935. The idea of moving Hareshowe to its new site was a popular one, and approved by all the official bodies involved.

Miss Barron remembered her excitement when, as a small child, she saw the carriage arrive in the summer of 1936. It was a third-class compartment, non-corridor LNER model, supplied by the Inverurie Loco Works at a cost of £20 plus the delivery charge. She watched as it was carefully lifted clear of the trailer by hand-operated jacks. When the trailer was pulled away the carriage was lowered one end at a time onto barrels, then half barrels, and finally on old railway sleepers.

Miss Barron's father and her Uncle Charlie then set about removing some of the partitions – all the seats had already been removed at the Loco Works – and painted the door white, in order to make it easier for her father, who had been partially blinded in the First World War, to find his way with feed or fertiliser. Two compartments were used to store these and when that was cleared out in the spring, chickens were reared within the carriage until they grew big enough to graduate to the hen house.

Chickens were favourite occupiers of such carriages. One of their neighbouring farmers would heave the chicken feed up onto the string luggage racks above the seats, leaving a door-open policy for his chickens, and opening the bag every day to allow a trickle of food to flow through, thus saving himself the constant bother of heaving a heavy feed sack into the hen house.

Miss Barron recalls one compartment was used as a bedroom when people came on holiday and the house was full up, and remembered sleeping there herself. 'It was a grand place if you didnae mind the smell of the hens, and equally braw for playing hoosies and shoppies.'

The area of Strathdon, Aberdeenshire, is about twenty-five miles west of Aberdeen. Look around Leochel Cushnie, Kildrummy, west to Strathdon village, and even beyond.

Major Innes and the misfired gun

Cowie House sits only a mile to the north of Stonehaven. For many generations it was inhabited by members of the Innes family. The *Baronage of Angus and the Mearns* reported that the first member of this family to live in or near the site of the present house was Walter de Innes, grandson and representative of Berowald the Fleming, the first of the family found upon record who obtained a charter from Malcolm IV: 'Berewaldo Flandrensi Innes at Easter Urcard' dated at Perth, Christmas 1155–56. He appears to be the progenitor of the Inneses of Scotland.

Cowie was once a village in its own right, separate from the adjoining town of Stonehaven, though no signpost indicates this today. The house now sits almost invisible behind a thick screen of trees, no doubt to provide privacy as well as to protect the inhabitants from the chill of an easterly wind. There is no inkling that the inhabitants wished for anything other than a quiet life.

But the railway still passes close to the rear of the house, as it has done for a hundred years or more. And to the immediate east of the house, along a well-defined footpath running no more than a quarter of a mile to a point over the cliffs, are three strange-looking, triangular, raised pieces of ground. These are now covered in turf, but the cut-stone foundations point to a substantial and careful construction.

There is little indication of their use. The iron seat placed in front of the centre structure indicates it as a place for visitors to sit and peacefully gaze out to sea. But peaceful their use was emphatically not. These were gun embrasures, although neither built nor used by any British army.

A local writer, Elizabeth Christie, wrote about the little village of Cowie in *The Empty Shore*, and described how the Innes who inherited the estate in 1863 was one Alexander Innes Esquire, of Cowie and Raemoir, and a major of the Artillery Volunteers. He was a soldier to the tips of his trigger-happy fingers, and apparently he recruited a number of men from the villages, whom he equipped with belts and swords. Upon the gun emplacements

Major Innes, who owned the land close to Stonehaven on which this gun emplacement is situated, enjoyed his very own 'Battery Brae' – firing cannonballs out to sea, and seriously not amusing Queen Victoria when she passed by on the train. He surprised her by firing a salute, much to her shock.

he had three guns sited, and built a powder magazine in a small hollow a little to the south (now invisible).

The point became known as Battery Brae, and on the sandstone cliff below, Innes had a hollow scooped out with steps leading out to it and a kind of a seat carved out of the rock. There he liked to sit and gaze across the bay, presumably while the guns were blazing overhead. Sadly, the Laird's Chair, as it was known, has disappeared through erosion by wind and weather.

But vivid memories of Major Innes' foibles live on. At one point he sent a young lad to Downie Point, across the bay, to note where the cannonballs landed. The first bounced home close to the poor boy's feet. The lad did not stay around to find out where the rest landed, but vanished at speed to the safety of the village.

Once, when Queen Victoria passed by train on her way to Balmoral, Innes ordered that a salute was to be fired in her honour. Unfortunately he omitted to mention this to Her Majesty or her retainers. By all accounts, a much shaken Queen Victoria was quite seriously unamused and, having been frightened out of her wits by the unexpected explosion, ordered that her extreme displeasure was to be passed on to Major Innes. History does not record his reaction to such a reprimand, but it seems to have done little to squash his somewhat overbearing character. When he took a drive through the village of Cowie the women would rush to gather in their washing from the line, the hanging-out of which Major Innes regarded as little short of a crime. One family who refused to conform had to move away.

The major's son, the Revd Disney Innes, was a gentle soul, a contrast to his father, whose love for all things military is well-remembered locally.

Cowie, Aberdeenshire, is one mile north of Stonehaven on the A92. The house can be found from the south by following signs to the golf course, past the Leisure Centre.

Royal trains

Today, the granite buildings of the former stations at Banchory and Aboyne still stand, although their use has changed. The

Deeside line ceased to function in the 1960s. The closure went ahead despite certain emergence of an oil boom in Aberdeen. However, 113 years prior to its closure, Queen Victoria was quick off the mark in her use of the new Deeside line. When, in 1853, she intimated that she would drive from Balmoral to Banchory to catch the train, she was unaware that Banchory Station was no more than a rough shed.

The railway company of the time recorded in a minute:

> Preparations for Her Majesty the Queen. It was resolved in consequence of Her Majesty having to pass along the line on the thirteenth instant, that she might require luncheon and accommodation at the station and the secretary should employ Mr Baird, upholsterer, to paper and paint the house occupied by the stationmaster for this purpose and supply whatever red cloth and carpeting as might be necessary.

When the queen came north the following year, a wooden refreshment room had been put up at Banchory and Her Majesty was entertained to lunch. The station was elaborately decorated, viewing stands were provided and the Banchory band was paid £2 to entertain the company. Since the station had few conveniences as yet – for example neither piped water nor gas – buckets of water and open fires must have been the order of the day, concealed from the royal and municipal guests.

The railway company counted the cost of the proceedings, and promptly decided to eliminate decorations in future, in order to cut down on cost. But by the time the railway reached Aboyne, they had undergone a change of heart, no doubt realising the potential revenue to be derived from a royal carriage steaming down the line. Aboyne got to work and erected stands on the station platform at the start of each season, selling seat space to a willing public.

Aboyne Station saw many royal visitors arrive and leave in the days before the railway reached Ballater. The sheriff once complained to the railway company about the large number of sightseers admitted to Aboyne platform, but Queen Victoria was never known to object. Perhaps she was unaware that the people in the stands were paying for the privilege of seeing her. And the railway company were adding the proceeds of the viewing seats to their profits.

Aboyne and Banchory, Grampian, are, respectively, about thirty and sixteen miles west of Aberdeen on the A93.

The gateway to Guthrie Castle

Of all the majestic castle entrances, the gateway to Guthrie Castle, with its small matching towers and castellated pediment, stands proudly among the best. It can be seen clearly today on the main Forfar/Friockheim road, a monument to nineteenth-century design, replacing, as it did, the former, more modest entrance which originally occupied the site.

Mr Guthrie of Guthrie Castle was rather pleased with his gatehouse when it was finished. The porter's lodge, however, was placed a short distance inside the main gateway, an unusual design, as generally a lodge would form part of the gate piers. The reason for the gap between the porter's lodge and the main gateway was simple. The gateway itself was actually an elaborate bridge for the railway line, which ran on top, and the porter's lodge was placed some distance away to lessen the noise and vibration which occurred when a train passed over.

This entrance gate to Guthrie Castle, doubling as it did as a railway bridge, sounds like an excellent example of landlord and railway company co-operation in a spirit of Victorian enterprise. Nothing could have been further from the truth.

The railway was regarded by landowners in the early days as an unpleasant intrusion on their privacy, and from this point of view they usually wanted it to be built as far away as possible from their land. On the other hand, they wanted it as close as possible for reasons of convenience. The two attitudes were often difficult to reconcile in practical terms.

When Mr Guthrie caught wind of the imminent arrival of the Arbroath to Forfar railway adjacent to his castle and policies, he was adamant. The railway line would have to run underground from a point ten feet before it reached the boundary of his estate. Faced with the problem of making a tunnel in flat meadowland,

The elaborate gateway to Guthrie Castle supports and hides the main railway line from Arbroath to Forfar.

the builders selected a new route, which took them outside the estate boundary. The disadvantage of this route was that the railway passed twice across the turnpike road within a very short distance, a process guaranteed to produce violent opposition from the turnpike trustees. The only way to avoid the turnpike was to push the railway hard against one of the existing Guthrie Castle entrances.

After prolonged negotiations, Mr Guthrie agreed to allow the railway to obliterate his gate, conditional on the railway company erecting a rather more grand new gate, incorporating a porter's lodge.

A Dundee architect drew up the plans, and the railway company reckoned that the cost would be £1,200. Horrified to find that the lowest tender for this elaborate railway bridge folly was £1,900, they solved the problem by shrewdly offering Mr Guthrie £1,400 to build his own gate, magnanimously suggesting that he could adjust the design if he so wished. Mr Guthrie accepted with alacrity, no doubt congratulating himself on his 'victory', and honour was satisfied all round.

The ivy-sheathed gateway was a landmark for passengers on the railway for nearly 130 years.

Guthrie, Angus. The gateway can be seen on the north side of the A932, about six miles east of Forfar, about halfway between Friockheim and Balgavies Loch.

6

Curious buildings with hidden lives

Boddin

It appears like a sinister, brooding castle, stuck on a promontory. In fact it's an outsize limekiln, built in the mid-eighteenth century by an ambitious young laird, Robert Scott of Dunninald and Rossie. It was his far-sighted ideas for agricultural improvements which led to the construction of this massive building, with its huge archways, giant openings through which the stones were tossed to be burnt in the fierce flames and reduced to valuable lime.

Brothers Patrick and Robert Scott came from a family of entrepreneurs. Their uncle sold salmon caught on this coast north of Lunan Bay to the good citizens of Venice; another kinsman had succeeded in selling 60,000 lobsters to London. Robert realised that by enclosing his fields, intensively cultivating and fertilising with lime, he would reap great benefits. This was, in 1696, an idea quite staggeringly ahead of its time.

Much of the story of the limekiln has been documented by John Stansfeld in *The Story of Dunninald*. He tells us that the east section of the building was the earliest to be built, and section after section of this immense pile was added over the next century. The scale of the building points to a competent and ambitious business brain, and the family fortunes rose in tandem. A description was given by traveller Francis Douglas in 1780. After ascending the steep hill from Lunan from the south, he arrived in an area which showed signs of 'improvement', by which he meant agricultural improvement. He described the good land, enclosed by whin hedges and roads which were broad and well made. But long before this, Robert Scott, one of the two brothers who had possessed the foresight to establish a limekiln and were the first agricultural innovators, perhaps in Scotland as a whole, died in

1697, along with his brother James, and since both were childless, their lands passed to Patrick.

But the limekiln, and the family fortunes, thrived. Patrick married in 1714, and his younger son, Robert, inherited Dunninald, the family property, in 1720. Robert married and proceeded to have five sons and seven daughters, and sounds a feisty soul, with an equally robust wife. Although there is a tale that Bonnie Prince Charlie spent his last night in a farmhouse in the area belonging to a Scott, it was unlikely that it was the house of Robert, as he had been a supporter of the Hanoverians. Indeed, when his life was threatened by Jacobites, it was his wife, pregnant with her twelfth child, who pleaded, successfully, for his life.

For a century and a half, the limekiln was ever productive. Vast amounts were produced, measured in the old Scots 'boll', the equivalent of 50 gallons; around 20 to 40 bolls would be required per acre to improve average soil.

To ensure that the limekiln could operate on maximum strength required the burning of copious quantities of coal, all of which had to be shipped in from the collieries in Fife. As the coal had to arrive by sea, and the lime depart by sea as well, a small harbour had to be constructed, and a pier with a sheltering cave into which boats are still stored to this day can not only be seen, but accessed easily. Montrose Town Council considered a notice on 16 April 1783 from Archibald Scott, of the third generation of the family, who was applying for government aid to construct the proposed pier at Boddin. The council supported him, along with a letter in favour written by ship masters. It is not known if this was ever successful, as the existing pier might predate this time. What is certain is that the ships which arrived earlier attached themselves to a mooring anchor 120 fathoms south-west of Boddin beach in 18 fathoms depth. John Stansfeld describes how an incoming vessel would attach itself to this mooring buoy at high tide and be hauled ashore until it was over the sandy beach. Lime would be put on board and she would lift off and sail away on the next tide. The system would be used with great care, as the beach was so exposed.

The following generation produced David Scott, who was perhaps the most successful of the Scotts, but his talents lay elsewhere. He became the MP for the area of Forfarshire in 1790, and chairman of the massive East India Company, and turned his sights on improving his policies at Dunninald. He employed architects Sir John Soane and James Playfair to draw up grandiose plans, few of which saw fruition. But what he did successfully accomplish was the repeal of excise duty on coal being shipped up the coast. Naturally this improved the profitability of his limekilns, but the elimination of the tax benefited the area, and his portrait by Romney commissioned by the town grandees hangs in the County Hall in Forfar.

So if you stroll down to inspect this crumbling edifice, turn sharp right to see a stone landing slip, leading into the cave into which fishing boats are dragged to this day. This is one of the very few salmon netting landing places left in Scotland. Visit at dusk, though, and it is only too easy to imagine this area as a smuggling haven, which indeed it also was a few hundred years ago. Robert Scott transformed the land into rich viable farmland, half a century before his ideas became popular. This small area has seen the generation of many fortunes, legal and entrepreneurial, as well as shifty and very much on the wrong side of the law.

Boddin, Angus, is on a small road about a mile from the A92, three miles as the crow flies south of Montrose. Great care should be taken when exploring the limekiln as much of this ancient piece of industrial heritage is crumbling.

Lady Charlotte's Cave

This is not marked on any map, but it is within a mile of the centre of Dunkeld, which is a tourist hot spot. The local tourist information office has little information on the cave, and finally, when you reach the official car park from which you venture up a well-marked track, not a trace of the cave is evident.

Lady Charlotte's Cave is a tiny folly so well camouflaged that it is possible to walk within a couple of metres of it and be unaware of its existence. The official path bypasses it, although another path diverts upwards, right past the cave's 'front door'. The cave is a cleft in the rocks which has been partially closed in with stones set in a latticework above the 'door' opening. Inside the L-shaped space is a stone bench or bed, and a fireplace with a chimney built up on the 'roof'. Enter the cave and the side entrance opens out onto a pool which is fed by its own waterfall and has been partially dammed by square-cut stones. It is the most perfect picnic spot. And that is indeed what it was, a hideaway picnic place for Lady Charlotte Murray, the daughter of the second Duke of Atholl, who married her first cousin John, who became the third duke. Charlotte and her husband had eleven children. Her portrait is in Blair Atholl Castle.

John, her husband, was an avid builder of follies – his most famous is the Hermitage on the Braan, near Dunkeld – and although no one knows who built this particular little refuge for Lady Charlotte, the odds must be that it was her husband. Both follies seem to have been built around the mid-eighteenth century. Theirs must have been a love match, as the death of John affected Charlotte deeply. In 1774 John and Charlotte and their children were living in the old Dunkeld House close by Dunkeld Cathedral. John was ill with a fever and was also inhaling smelling salts. Waking up, he grabbed what he thought was water, but in fact it turned out to be the smelling salts dissolved in water. Crazed with thirst and fever, the story tells, he staggered down the few metres to the River Tay, where he fell in and drowned. Charlotte was distraught, and left, taking her eleven children with her. She never returned to Dunkeld.

Dunkeld is twelve miles north of Perth on the A9. Take the road through Dunkeld to the A923 signposted east to Blairgowrie. A mile from the centre of Dunkeld, turn up a very rough track and follow signs for the Cally car park. Take the walk just behind the display board, and about a fifteen-minute walk further on, clamber over a fallen yew tree. Soon after this, turn sharp right up a lesser footpath and the cave is within a few metres.

Kildrummy Church or meal mill?

From the outside, Kildrummy Church has a slight air of uncertainty about it. Did the building have an identity crisis at some point in its history? It is tempting to imagine more than a touch of Aberdonian shrewdness about the mill-like appearance of this country kirk. Were the plans mixed up, or did the building start out as a mill and end up as a kirk? Who knows. The ancient story of the area adds much of interest to what could just be conjecture.

The site on which Kildrummy Kirk stands has been occupied from the very earliest times. It was formerly surrounded on three sides by water, which made it an ideal defensive position. The prominence of the site would commend itself to the religious as well as the civil authorities of past ages and it is likely that it may have been the scene of even pre-Druidic religious rites.

Little is known of the early days of Christianity in Kildrummy, but there are dedications to St Machar, St Ronan, St Moluag and St Mary, all within a few miles of the kirk. The dedication of the kirk itself is not too well authenticated but it is thought to have been to St Bride and that is the name by which the kirk is known today. However, it is also known that in 581, Brude, King of the Picts, founded here a chapel dedicated to St Bennet. Bennet's name has not survived nor is the site of his chapel known. But it is possible that the king's chapel was erected on the present site, which is only a few hundred yards from the site of the prehistoric fortress. And it may be that Brude's name has been corrupted into Bride.

Although built on the site of an ancient place of worship, and indeed constructed from stones of a previously ruined church, local gossip still reckons that the plans were for a meal mill, which it much resembles, rather than a church.

The interior of Kildrummy Church.

The ruined church on top of the mound was built not later than 1335. The custom was always to build on ground already hallowed or consecrated, so it is likely that there was an earlier ecclesiastical building – perhaps Brude's chapel or its immediate successor. The medieval church was known also as the Chapel of Lochs, because of its surroundings.

A few hundred yards from the kirk beside the approach road is a small hillock known as the Bell Knowe. On the ancient dead tree which still stands on the Knowe, the bells of the medieval church were hung.

In 1605 the Elphinstone lairds of Kildrummy built the kirk porch, which still stands complete. It was used as a burial aisle by the Elphinstones and there are a number of interesting old stones in the buildings. In 1805 the present church was erected largely from the stones of the ancient church. It is still popularly held that it was put together from plans for a meal mill, but the interior gives no doubts about the building's function. This is a much-loved church.

The ancient font near the pulpit predates the present building by many centuries, dating from about 1330.

Kildrummy, Aberdeenshire. Take the A944 from Aberdeen for thirty-three miles until the junction with the A97. Turn left. The kirk can be seen on the south side of the road within a couple of miles.

The hidden Deeside hamlets of Glen Muick

With all the massive amounts of documentation about Upper Deeside and its connection with the royal family, and Balmoral in particular, it is difficult to believe that there could be a stone of the area unexplored. But there are several. Even devotees of the hills would be hard put to it to know where the deserted village of Blackandge is located. Even more surprising is its proximity to the main Glen Muick road, and its views towards the late Queen Mother's Deeside residence of Birkhall.

The position of the main ruined village, Blackandge, is OS NO357925. You can see the main houses clustered higgledy-piggledy around the water lade, with its large slabs of stone covering the lade in parts. Following this lade round the contour of the hill to the south and then swinging round to the east, another smaller set of buildings includes a limekiln. These are of later date and could possibly have been used in the nineteenth century.

The larger village shows evidence of broad sinuous rigs and furrows, possibly 500 to 600 years old. Ian Shepherd, a Grampian regional archaeologist, reckons that this village and the surrounding area were used for periods and then abandoned and then re-occupied and eventually used for a more pastoral form of farming, for example sheep-farming.

The village is marked on General Roy's military survey map of 1750, but only a rig is there on Robertson's map of 1823. Why the village was used, then abandoned, then used again is a mystery. Almost nothing is known about the area. But adding further to the mystery and seclusion of this habitation is the curious area of ground almost due north of the main village. Upon a raised triangular piece of ground, close to where the water lade falls into two successive ponds – which look man-made – are indentations in the ground at irregular intervals. They are circular, hollowed out like a large saucer shape, some still showing evidence of stabilising with stones round the perimeter. They are too small apparently for pre-medieval huts, and the theory that they could have been used as burial places is unlikely, as there is no previous evidence of this. It is a place of mystery indeed.

To find this gem of a hidden village, take the B976 south-west from the bridge at Ballater, and turn off left to the Glen Muick road. Follow the road no more than two miles, passing Birkhall, until on a straight piece of road you see a burn and small bridge. Park in the roadman's layby immediately north of this, and follow the burn up the hill, turning north a little. The distance from the centre of Ballater to the parking place is three miles. Ordnance Survey map reference NO357925.

Mary King's Close

Stand in Cockburn Street in the Old Town of Edinburgh and gaze up at the magnificent rear of the City Chambers. Look to the right-hand side and let your eye follow down the lines of symmetrical windows. One window is not altogether as it should be. In fact it is not really a window at all, but an opening covered with an iron grille. This is the end of Mary King's Close, one of the myriad of closes now hidden from view, but not, like so many of the others, lost forever.

It is not a straightforward process to take a walk down Mary King's Close. Go up to the High Street and there is no sign of it. It is not on the usual tourist routes, nor can you arrange a visit during the day. Evening visits only are allowed. A special arrangement with the City Chambers, who will organise a guide for special groups, numbering no more than a dozen or so, is the method of access.

You are taken into a side entrance to the City Chambers, and then a door opens and down, down the stairs you go. Mary King's Close is only a couple of floors high, and all that remains of a medieval tenement. A close is and was a narrow road between two towering blocks of buildings. Many examples can still be seen in Edinburgh. This close, now roofed over with the ground floor of the City Chambers, was once open to the sky, and soared eleven storeys high.

The close is about sixty metres long and not much more than two metres wide. Not surprisingly, it is also very steep, dropping eighteen metres from top to bottom, and once continued down into the Nor Loch (it actually was a loch, with a ferryman who plied his trade across), which, now filled in, has become Princes Street Gardens and Waverley Station.

Mary King's Close is not for the claustrophobic, but definitely for those who believe in ghosts, those fascinated by history, and those whose appetite for polished-up stately homes is tired and sated. To enter Mary King's Close is to enter the shadows of history. Few people walk nowadays on the old brick pavements, and the dust you disturb with your twentieth-first-century shoes will settle just as it did 500 years ago over generations of bare feet. No concession in the normal 'tourist' sense is given to the visitor. There are no signs, except those pointing to fire exits, and they exist primarily for workmen servicing the miles of pipes and wires running around.

There is a bakehouse, no more than one and a half metres wide, with huge ovens and proving trays of slabs of stone. Great vaulted rooms which were once used as shops, then bricked over at one end, had a reincarnation as bomb shelters during the Second World War.

Inside these vaulted areas, traders included a butcher and a wine merchant, and you can still see the hooks and remains of a pulley where the latter would haul his wine barrels up.

One 'house', or ground-floor flat, has its front door opening onto Mary King's Close and its back door onto Anchor Close. These houses were narrow, and Deacon Brodie, that respectable burglar who has entered Edinburgh folklore, could, like others of his ilk, vanish into a house, pass through into another close and 'disappear'.

Inside are the remains of stencilled walls, blackened marks on the room where the box beds were set, and a small smart parlour with wooden floorboards – as opposed to dirt floors – and a tiny fireplace. Up to the left above the fireplace is a section where the wall has been hacked open, and then clumsily filled up with bricks again. This, says the guide, is where the chimney sweep was stuck and they had to dismantle part of the wall in order to free him. Was he dead or alive? No one seems to be sure, but his ghost cries out into the room sometimes, and others speak of a small girl in green sitting on a stool by the fire.

To top these tales, in more senses than one, is the knowledge that above you rises the entire structure of the City Chambers building, supported on the foundations of this dry, solid village.

But why does this close still exist? The origins lie in the bubonic plague of 1645, which cut a swathe through the population of Edinburgh and this close in particular. Then it was named Alexander King's Close, as he was the owner at that time (the names of closes generally changed with the owner). Almost all the inhabitants of this close died, including Alexander King's daughter, Mary. When the plague abated, the people who had fled the plague or escaped its clutches crept back, but never into this close. It was haunted, they said, by Mary King. She is still there, needless to say, but a quiet, friendly soul, who just waits and watches.

She must have had a long wait in order to see much of interest, as the close was completely sealed up and ignored until a fire in 1750. Shortly after that the top storeys were sliced off and the Royal Exchange was built between 1753 and 1761. And so Mary King's Close, with its seething populace, its warren of houses, shops and ale houses, its gutter which carried the refuse of dozens of homes and businesses, was permanently sealed up and almost forgotten.

Mary King's Close is in the Old Town of Edinburgh. See the text for details of how to visit the close.

Pickletillum: What's in a name?

The former Pickletillum Inn (now a private house), on the Dundee/Cupar road, used to be the last stop of the Edinburgh

This unique name appears to be derived from the exhortations of a mid-eighteenth-century joiner to his apprentice to 'add a pickle more nails for my money'.

stagecoach. There must be a good reason for the curious name, which is not just bizarre but possibly unique. The front-runner for the true story behind the name runs as follows ...

Around the mid-eighteenth century, the local joiner used to send his lad out to the blacksmith for a supply of nails, and was constantly displeased with the amount he received for his money. It was his retort to his lad that next time around he should add 'a pickle til 'em' (add a pickle more for the money) that in due course gave the joiner his nickname, and this in turn gave the whole area its name.

Much later, the inn was established and the then owner, a Mr Veitch, was a special constable at Pickletillum. He had to use his baton on one occasion in an attempt to turn back people fleeing from the cholera plague which threatened Dundee. Sadly, this desperate attempt failed to stem the flow of people or the tracks of the epidemic. The people who were afflicted and now lie in a mass grave in Forgan churchyard testify to the virulence of the disease.

The former Pickletillum Inn, Fife, lies on the east side of the A914, just three miles south of the Tay Road Bridge, and three miles north of Leuchars.

Miss Maggie Gruer's walkers' rest house

Inverey, on the secondary road west from Braemar, Aberdeen-shire, is a hamlet which has produced at least two outstanding characters. John Lamont left home at a very early age and never returned, but the village has a large memorial to his achievements. Almost opposite the memorial is Thistle Cottage, the home of Miss Maggie Gruer, who lived all her life in Inverey. Her memorial, in the shape of her fireside chair, now supports the seat of the president of the Cairngorm Club.

John Lamont was born on 13 December 1805, and left home at the tender age of twelve to enter the Scots Benedictine College at Ratisbon (Regensburg) in Germany, but upon graduation rejected a life in the Church and entered Munich University in 1828. In 1830 he was appointed assistant at the Royal Observatory near Munich, five years later becoming director of the institution and finally being made professor in 1852. He was created a knight of the Order of Merit of the Bavarian Crown and died on 6 August 1870.

Notice of Lamont's death caught the eye of the Crown Princess of Germany, Vicky, who was the eldest daughter of Queen Victoria and Prince Albert. She sent the press cuttings to her mother, and it was discovered that Johann von Lamont's relatives still lived in Upper Deeside. His achievements are briefly detailed on the memorial on the south side of the road.

Miss Maggie Gruer's claim to fame was in many ways equally widespread, as into her home and to her fireside flocked hikers from all walks of life, and in all states of exhaustion. She also came to the notice of the royal family when she wrote to the papers – or, writing not being her strong point, asked someone to write for her – and her letter, objecting to attempts to prevent local folk taking in paying guests, was allegedly read out in the House of Commons. The king heard of this and was furious that Inverey folks should be prevented from taking in visitors and Maggie upheld that 'he fairly danced when he heard aboot it'.

Her father, James, farmed the croft and when her mother was not working on the croft, the ladies gave hospitality to hill walkers. After her husband's death, Maggie's mother continued to work the croft and put up hill walkers, until her death in 1909.

Maggie then continued the tradition. She loved meeting people and the feeling was mutual. Walkers just down from the hills, wet, hungry and in need of shelter before continuing on the final path home, were invited into her snug 'room' with its box bed, and treated to tea from a pot that seemed to be endlessly refilled, as well as her home-made bannocks and eggs from the hens at the back door. Hikers could doss down in many corners of the small house, but also, if all other places were occupied, in the barn at the back. Maggie was a good listener and a better talker, entertaining visitors with tales of Queen Victoria and John Brown.

She charged them all, having no truck with those who tried to wriggle out of their dues, and was very forthright in her demands for the amounts of cash she requested. The majority signed their names in her visitor 'bookies', and after her death these, along with her favourite fireside chair, were given to Hugh Welsh, a Cairngorm Club committee member for sixty years, and an honorary president of the club from 1955 to 1969. The books are now properly bound, titled and housed in the Cairngorm Club library. Born in 1861, Maggie Gruer died in 1939.

Inverey, Aberdeenshire, is about sixty miles due west from Aberdeen. Follow first the A93 to Braemar then the secondary road due west to Inverey for the last five miles.

Aberlour orphanage

The tower standing guard over a pile of rubble in Aberlour has watched over generations of children. Today, it views the children

Canon Charles Jupp became a legend in his own lifetime. He founded an orphanage and spent his life fighting the prevalent Victorian belief that all poor children were 'tainted with the pauperism'.

So successful were successive heads of the Aberlour Orphanage in wheedling money out of the landed gentry that they were also rewarded with royal visits. Here King George V and Queen Mary are shown visiting the orphanage in the 1920s.

of the Speyside High School, but for nearly 100 years, the tower viewed successions of 'orphans'.

But the chances are that while most people have heard of Barnardo's and the Quarrier Homes, the majority will have never heard of the Aberlour Orphanage.

Founded in 1875 by an Anglican clergyman, the Revd Charles Jupp, Aberlour opened its doors at roughly the same time as homes founded by Dr Barnardo, Quarrier and Muller. This was the time of the great flowering of Victorian social conscience and philanthropy. Unlike these other institutions, the Aberlour Orphanage never grew to anything like their huge scale.

By the early part of the twentieth century, 500 children had become the declared maximum and this was never exceeded, even though demand up to the Second World War could have permanently doubled its population. As a result, Aberlour never became the 'children business' which characterised other institutions of the same ilk, nor did it achieve the familiarity or fame of Dr Barnardo's.

The refectory at the Aberlour Orphanage served up simple, staple fare to generations of children. Much of the produce consumed was home-grown.

In its heyday, the Aberlour Orphanage, complete with its own 'houses',
school, farm, sanatorium and workshops, housed 500 children.

Tucked away from the mainstream of the world, with its own
farm and school, life was based on the rhythm of frequent church-
going. The form of worship was Episcopalian, and this in an area
of uncompromising Presbyterianism.

Canon Charles Jupp came from Newcastle where, after years of
working in the slums, his health had collapsed. He had accepted
the invitation of Miss McPherson Grant of Aberlour House (now
a preparatory school with close associations with Gordonstoun) to
be her chaplain, provided she agreed to the funding of a church
in the village (St Margaret's, still standing) and the building of an
orphanage.

Only a couple of years after the orphanage opened, disaster
struck the project when Miss McPherson Grant died at the age
of forty-three. Worse, her estate became the subject of a legal
battle. This was between Miss Temple, former companion of
Miss McPherson Grant, and Miss Temple's ex-husband. Miss
Temple and Miss McPherson Grant had what was probably a
form of lesbian relationship, having undergone a 'marriage' in

the library of Aberlour House, conducted by the local Presbyterian minister.

Captain Yeatman, the former husband of Miss Temple, now contested the will on the grounds that, as a 'marriage' had taken place, so therefore his former wife was entitled to half the value of Miss McPherson Grant's estate, but he lost this case in the House of Lords.

Notwithstanding these setbacks, the orphanage continued to thrive. Canon Jupp secured money from any source he could. Stories abound of him sitting on trains knitting socks for the children, and he is known to have personally cut out and sewed their clothes.

He would travel the country offering to preach for the local rector, if he could include an appeal for the orphanage in his sermon. Kneeling down in the church at Aberlour, his tattered shoes and socks were revealed to the wealthy landowning congregation, and he hoped this would shame them into donating to the orphanage.

Jupp was loud in his criticism of the existing system whereby a child could be returned to his parents if they so desired, which frequently meant for prostitution or begging purposes. He scoffed at the 'right of the parent' to reclaim a child despite obvious ill-treatment. He was also an outspoken believer in the ability of a child to grow up and flourish in society, notwithstanding his origins of birth, an unpopular idea at the time. He ridiculed the oft-spoken description of 'his' children that they had the 'pauper' taint and could never rise above this in later life.

To his orphanage came children of all ages. And all through the history of the orphanage, children remembered most vividly their arrival and very early life there. Here are a few of their diary notes.

1897

There were three of us boys. My Mum had cancer and was dying, although at that time we just knew that she was getting ill all the time. So my Dad brought us up from England and left us with our Mum and her parents in Edinburgh. He scarpered and I never saw him again. After a while my middle brother and myself were sent off by train to a place called the Aberlour Orphanage. I was six years old.

We settled down quite easily, I suppose. After all, it wasn't much of a home that we had left. About three years later we were sent down to see my Mum. She was lying on a bed and could not speak. I didn't recognise her, and hardly knew the rest of the family, not that they paid much attention to us. We sat beside her for what seemed hours, and then were put back on a train to the Orphanage. A little while after that we received a letter telling us that she had died. I went outside and had a cry for a few minutes. It seemed expected of me. The next day I had forgotten all about her.

1920

My mother died the day that I was born, on the 21st of April 1920. I was put into the Orphanage at three weeks old and left in 1939.

My earliest memories are of a Miss Davidson, a big, tall woman from Ballindalloch who I called Daisen. She was in charge of the little ones, but one day she had gone. She was really too old to cope with us toddlers and had been sent to the sewing room where she spent most of her time darning socks.

I was furious, and somehow one day got hold of a darning needle and went round pricking people with it. I was cross that she had to darn socks rather than pay attention to me. I stopped eating. I was too young to go to school. No one knew what to do with me.

The next thing was that I was taken up to stay with her in the sewing room to be close to her, and the crisis was over...

Years later, I married a boy from the Orphanage, it was the first wedding there. It was wartime, and they pulled out all the stops for us, rationing or no.

1946

I can remember the day clearly, the 2nd July 1946, it was a Tuesday. I could take you to the same bus now. Mother told the six of us that we were going off for the day on holiday, although it was a school day.

It was early, about 8, a lovely, sunny day and we were all dressed up in our best clothes. We went to a court house. Dean Wolfe was there and two others from the Orphanage.

We were taken into a room one by one and asked questions about our home life, for example, 'Did you attend school, did your mother stay out late?' Then, eventually how would we like to go to a place where there are lots of other boys and girls? We thought, this sounds exciting, and said yes.

We were taken outside, the four youngest, and jumped in this big, black car. On the drive there Dean Wolfe was very cheery and gave us sweeties, told us funny stories about his dog Spey, which did lots of tricks. All true. We thought that it was all great fun, off to a holiday, off to a holiday camp or suchlike.

But when we were driven away, there was my Mum crying and shouting on the pavement and very, very upset. Now I realise that the court made its decision there and then and we were separated from my mother, all because she had another baby during the war when my Pa was away.

After Canon Jupp's death, the orphanage was led by a succession of three more Episcopal rectors who followed, more or less, the initial philosophy of raw-boned Christianity combined with an ability to charm the higher social echelons to part with their money. Financially, this was a successful combination.

The word 'orphanage' could be a misnomer. A few of the children were indeed true orphans, but many more were dispatched to Aberlour because they had been abandoned by their parents, were illegitimate (from both ends of the social scale) or boarded out and paid for by what are now referred to as one-parent families. This social mix was common to all the major orphanages.

Acquiring money to feed and clothe the brood was in itself a major part of the warden's job. Charles Jupp, his determination sharpened by empty larders, took to begging early on: from pulpits, in his letters, trudging from door to door. Described to his face as the 'great Northern beggar', he seriously suggested that his epitaph should be 'at last the beggar died'.

His giant jumble sales drew eager clients with bundles of empty pillow cases from as far afield as Aberdeen, Peterhead and Inverness. They were finally christened for posterity in local parlance as 'the Jupps'.

Most children on leaving the orphanage were found work in the area. Not for Aberlour the mass shipping of children off to the Dominions, as Barnardo's did. Despite the majority of the children's birthplaces being in the big cities, lots chose to stay put in the area after they left. Many more crept back to live close by. Aberlour kept a hostel in part of the orphanage for returning 'children' for whom life outside had turned sour. Another workplace was sometimes found for them, but in the meantime the prodigal stray earned his or her keep in the laundry, kitchen or garden.

The orphanage closed its doors in 1967. Society viewed institutional upbringing as old-fashioned, and the Aberlour Child Care Trust, which exists today, bought small houses in the main cities of Scotland, and children lived in a more homely atmosphere. The children were dispersed carefully to smaller homes around Scotland, closer to relatives, so that family contact could be maintained. The building was sold and so were the contents, amid shrieks of fury at the give-away prices realised for what had been donated and hard-won over the years. Eventually the building was demolished.

Apart from the church which stands aloof and unchanged, there is little to remind returning Aberlour children of their home. The church congregation is decimated, its visitors' book crowded with the signatures of returning 'orphans'.

On the rubble-strewn site of the orphanage there remains only the original clock-tower. The adjacent walls have all been torn away and the uneven lower edges of stone are all neat and restored. Some photographs of the orphanage are to be seen in the old station waiting room, along with photographs of Aberlour in the last century.

Aberlour, also known as Charlestown of Aberlour, Moray, is thirteen miles south of Elgin on the A941. The tower of the orphanage is visible on the south side of the main street, at the north-east edge of the town, near St Margaret's Church.

Tarfside Tower

St Andrew's Tower, or Tarfside Tower, on Modlach Hill, Glen Esk, stands proud on the hillside, easily visible to the passing walker. This is exactly why it was erected, a year after a tragic accident.

In January 1827, the Revd Jolly, the Episcopalian rector from Tarfside, and his companion, a Miss Douglas, were caught in a blizzard in the glen. They were returning home from a wedding at the Mill of Auchean. They lost their bearings in the storm and, sadly, Miss Douglas perished before they were found.

In 1828, the Masonic Lodge erected the tower to guide walkers on the surrounding moorland. In 1971 the compass and square on the top of the tower were repaired. The procession of the Lodge of St Andrew's no longer marches over to the tower on St Andrew's Day, as it once did.

Tarfside Tower, Angus. Take the B966 from Brechin north to Edzell. Just north of Edzell take the secondary road left and north to Glen Esk. About eight miles further on the tower is visible from the road. Ordnance Survey map reference NO525786.

Steele and Brodie, bee-keepers for the nation

On the very edge of Wormit in Fife, along the Kilmany Road, amid a row of suburban houses, stood a rather ramshackle collection of buildings which were Steele and Brodie's manufacturing base. Almost everything connected with the fascinating business of bee-keeping was sold there. Behind this unprepossessing façade hid a fascinating business story more than a century old.

The founder of this business, Robert Steele, was in the 1860s an enquiring teenager, living in the village of Fowlis Easter in Angus. He was given as a present a skep of bees, and as his stock

Beginners' Outfits.

We shall be pleased to give instructions and advice to intending beginners in Beekeeping.

These outfits include everything necessary for a beginner.—Other appliances can be secured as need for them arises.

THE "UNIVERSAL" OUTFIT.

No. 2 Hive, with wired Foundation in Frames and Full Sheets in Sections.

Feeder.
Queen Excluder.
Smoker and Fuel.
Veil.
Quilts.
Porter Escape and Board.
Book on Beekeeping.

Price, 60/-, carriage paid.

THE "STANDARD" OUTFIT.

No. 8 New Standard W.B.C. Hive, with 2 crates of Sections, wired Foundation in Frames and Full Sheets in Sections.

Feeder.
Queen Excluder.
Smoker and Fuel.
Veil.
Quilts.
Porter Escape and Board.
Book on Beekeeping.

Price 85/-, carriage paid.

Either of above painted, 6/- extra.

BEES.—Specially selected strain of Bees if ordered with above outfit.

French Package Bees ... at 35/- extra.
On 6 Frames, ... at 60/- extra.
On 8 Frames, ... at 70/- extra.

SAFE DELIVERY GUARANTEED (see Page 74).

Any other Hive in catalogue can be substituted at difference in catalogue price.

Awarded First Prize at Highland Show, Glasgow, 1934, and Bronze Medal, Crystal Palace, 1934.

An innovation in the 1860s, Robert Steele's wooden beehives replaced the traditional straw skeps which had housed bees for thousands of years. Steele went on to found his own successful workshop in Wormit, Fife.

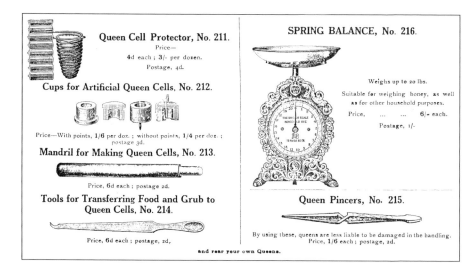

Queen Cell Protector, No. 211.

Price—
4d each ; 3/- per dozen.
Postage, 4d.

Cups for Artificial Queen Cells, No. 212.

Price—With points, 1/6 per doz. ; without points, 1/4 per doz. ; postage 3d.

Mandril for Making Queen Cells, No. 213.

Price, 6d each ; postage 2d.

Tools for Transferring Food and Grub to Queen Cells, No. 214.

Price, 6d each ; postage, 2d,

and rear your own Queens.

SPRING BALANCE, No. 216.

Weighs up to 20 lbs.

Suitable for weighing honey, as well as for other household purposes.

Price, ... 6/- each.

Postage, 1/-

Queen Pincers, No. 215.

By using these, queens are less liable to be damaged in the handling.

Price, 1/6 each ; postage, 2d.

By the end of the 19th century every aspect of bee-keeping was catered for in Steele and Brodie's workshop, as this catalogue illustrates.

of bees increased, so he turned his hand to making more and more bee skep in which to nurture his flock. But his inventive mind turned to the possibility of making a wooden hive. By now he had become apprenticed as a millwright in his father's workshop, and it was there he began experimenting with commercially saleable wooden hives. The only other wooden hive made at this time was an octagonal one from Ayrshire, the only other thriving pocket of bee-keeping in Scotland at that time.

Working long after his very lengthy working day ended, Robert Steele began to pick up orders. Transport difficulties were overcome by persuading the local baker to transport the hives to the nearest railway station, lashed to the roof of his van. By the time of the first show of the Scottish Bee-keepers Association in 1876, Robert Steele's hives carried off all the prizes, and continued to do so for many years.

In time, Robert Steele's enterprise outgrew his father's workshop. He moved his workshop to Gauldry, nearby in Fife, until a disastrous fire wiped it out. The new works he built on the Kilmany Road lasted for a hundred years.

Mr Brodie became a partner at the turn of the century, and the business was in the ownership of the Robertson family until 1981. At one point, just after the First World War, the firm expanded their range to the making of poultry houses and any general joinery work. But the huge increase of interest in bee-keeping between the wars meant that all sidelines were discontinued and the firm concentrated solely on their main business of manufacturing for bee-keeping. This specialism continued until the end of the business in Fife in the late 1990s.

The majority of bee-keepers – and Steele and Brodie's catalogues flew out in their thousands to customers all over the UK and Ireland – regarded their bee-keeping as a hobby. Few of them made a living from producing honey, owing to the vagaries of the British summer weather. But other forms of farming encouraged bee-keeping. For example, the upsurge in raspberry growing in the mid-Perthshire areas stimulated bee-keeping as an excellent method of pollinating the crops.

Gradually other bee-keeping businesses disappeared until, after 1945, Steele and Brodie stood almost alone. They scored another coup when they secured the sole agency for that essential wax for bees, called Dadents.

The firm strove for more business. Bees of a 'calm temperament' were imported from France, to be sent north by train. However, all was not calm at the Dover docks, as some of the bees made good their escape as soon as they hit terra firma. Leaping on a plane, Mr Robertson, senior member of the Fife firm, arrived at the docks to be hustled through in record time to deal with the situation. In due course, he was ushered onto the train with his precious cargo of bees, now recaptured, only to be ordered to stay with them in the guard's van. Neither the customs officers nor British Rail would take undue risks.

Bee-keeping is a low-profile but flourishing form of farming and the enterprise of Robert Steele and his successors survived for over a century. Heather honey was, and still is, one of the most sought-after forms of honey, and demand far exceeds supply. Although new sources have aided production (oil seed rape, for example, with its early flowers, has filled a gap in the early season when there are few other flowers to attract bees), they will not replace the appeal of clover honey, which has declined in line with the decline in cattle-rearing on farms – fewer clover fields means less clover honey, an unfortunate knock-on effect in the cycle of farming.

The former beehive works of Steele and Brodie are situated on the B946 out of Wormit, Fife, going south, now replaced with a modern housing development.

The Grey Cairns of Camster

The Grey Cairns of Camster sit on boggy land on a straight, unnamed road running between Occumster and Watten, a distance of about fifteen miles. The road features on no tourist route. You would be unlikely to meet more than a handful of cars if you drove on it all day long. The site of the cairns is clearly marked, and they are cared for by Historic Scotland, but even today the mystery of their presence is still partially unsolved. Initially, the onlooker is baffled as to why such seemingly random stone structures lie in the middle of this boggy area.

The piles of stones, about four metres high, at first sight could be an 'installation' in a very modern art gallery. Peer closely, and you can see that the stones are not placed randomly; in fact they look as though they could indeed be a work of art, piled with meticulous care.

Where did all these stones come from? Were they dragged many miles, and if so how? After all, the ground itself is so soft that walking is tricky enough, let alone rolling stones over long distances.

You can crawl into these cairns, and there is just about room to stand upright inside. As you do, pause for a moment, to reflect that you are standing in a creation which is at least 5,000 years old. The cairns date from the Neolithic Age, and the long cairn to the right of your vision was, according to Historic Scotland, a complex structure with forecourts each end, and, incredibly, encasing two structures of even greater antiquity.

Camster Round was initially explored in the 1850s and '60s, and its chamber was found to be virtually intact. There are various reports and descriptions of what was found. Some reports say that human skeletons were discovered, sitting upright, others just refer to a large amount of human bone, animal bone and pottery. There was also evidence of burning in the centre of the chamber, where quantities of charcoal and ash were particularly abundant.

Why were these constructions sited in what today looks like the centre of a bleak, windswept bog, with the modern addition of the inevitable Sitka spruce trees? Perhaps there is beauty in this landscape, but little in the way of comfort and no evident way of earning a living.

The answer lies in the many changes which have taken place in the landscape over the last 5,000 years. At the time the cairns were built the immediate area enjoyed a good climate and the land was far more fertile than it appears today. The builders of these structures were farmers, growing wheat and raising cattle and sheep, and the cairns were on the edge of their farmland. The landscape would have been much more attractive, with plenty of trees, which provided shelter and vital nutrients to the soil. As the ground was tilled and exploited during the Bronze Age, the topsoil was eroded, a disastrous consequence for the fertility of the soil, which was washed away, with heavy rainfalls destroying further the unprotected soil.

Continue on this road northwards and you will see modern-day farms, the fields frequently edged with waist-high slabs of Caithness stone, used in centuries past as fencing.

Camster can be reached by taking an unmarked road on the left at Occumster, which is five miles north of Latheron on the A99. This road eventually arrives at Watten. The Grey Cairns are about halfway along, around six miles from the turn-off.

7

Farming folk and water-borne tales

Robert Nicoll, farmer's son

The obelisk behind Tullybelton Farm stands on a little hillock, its superb block stone and workmanship visible from the A9 about four miles north of Perth. This memorial is in honour of a farmer's son who saved up 1*s*. 6*d*. to join the local library when it opened in Bankfoot on 25 January 1827, and rose to become a poet, political radical, bookshop owner, and editor of the *Leeds Times* by the age of twenty-two. In his day Robert Nicoll was hailed as the worthy successor to Robert Burns and a youthful prodigy. The obelisk was raised by his friends as a tribute to a remarkable young man, who was just twenty-three years old when he died.

Born on 7 January 1814, Robert Nicoll was a son of ordinary farming folk, owners of Little Tullybelton until their bankruptcy, which occurred when young Robert was six years old. His parents were modest, but quietly influential in his life. They were early supporters of the Seceders within the Church and defied their landlord, the Honourable Margaret Nairne, in her demand that the family should attend the new Episcopal chapel she had built. On receiving a flat refusal, the lady threatened them with eviction, but Mrs Nicoll replied that, 'The land we have is your ain, and ye may do as ye like wi't, but I'll no gang to your chapel.'

The Nicolls encouraged their children to read early and obtain as much education as they could, despite their poverty. At the age of four Robert was poring over his copy of the New Testament, brought home from Peter Hill of Perth and bound with 'fragrant sheep leather, and garnished with a lion and unicorn and the imprint of Sir David Hunter Blair'. At twelve he was reading the Waverley Novels. His schooling continued intermittently, culminating in the winter of 1829 when he went for a final six weeks to Mr Porter's school at Moneydie.

The memorial obelisk to young newspaper editor and poet Robert Nicoll at Tullybelton, north of Perth. It is inscribed with his words 'I have written my poetry in my heart'.

Of Nicoll's four schoolteachers, two were published poets, which may explain his early love of poetry. Of all the skills which Robert packed into his twenty-three years, poetry appears to have been his first and strongest love. As the inscription on his obelisk says: 'I have written my poetry in my heart'.

But much other writing was to be produced by him on his way to being a poet. He needed to earn a living, and, in view of the family's poverty, he had to start early. At the age of thirteen he was appointed Bankfoot correspondent for the local Perth newspaper. Aged seventeen he left home and was indentured to Mrs James Hay Robertson, a grocer on the south side of the High Street in Perth. Although he appreciated her as a just and fair employer, his sights were set much further afield. One of his long-term plans included saving enough to sail for America. In the meantime, he became embroiled in politics, as a Radical very much in opposition to the Tories in power, and was soon to see the first of his stories in print, in *Johnstone's Magazine*.

By the age of twenty Nicoll had managed to borrow the money to open a bookshop and lending library in Dundee, but this was only moderately successful as his heart was not in the business of shopkeeping and his waking hours were packed with writing and politics. Young as he was, he became a weel-kent figure in Dundee, noted for his piercing eyes and commanding presence, as well as for his shabby dress – he was once taken to task by a friend about the appearance of his only coat, which had a sleeve attached by only a couple of threads. Sadly, despite vivid contemporary descriptions, not a single drawing of him exists.

Shabby clothing notwithstanding, Nicoll was an imposing enough character to attract the attention of several publishers, who were more than willing to risk printing his poems. They were not to be disappointed. Reprint after reprint sold out.

Nicoll's best poems, simple, lyrical and full of feeling, are written in Scots dialect. 'The Grandfather' reflects his early influences:

Thy daily fireside worship dwells
Within this inmost soul of mine,
Thy earnest prayer sae prophet-like
For aa on earth I wadna tyne.
But mair than that – frae books sae auld,
Frae mony treasured earnest
Thou traced for me the march of truth,
The path of right from age to age,

A peasant, auld, and puir and deaf,
Bequeathed this legacy to me;
I was his bairn – he filled my soul.

Aside from his passionate involvement with politics, Nicoll was
falling in love, and expressed himself thus:

A leal young heart's first love is better than it aa
Sic love was never tauld in sangs,
Sic sangs were never sung.

At the age of twenty he married a Dundee lass, Alice Gray.

Ah thought on aa the tales, Alice
O woman's love and faith,
Of truth that smiled at fear, Alice,
And love that conquered death.
Affection blessing hearts and homes
When joy was far awa,
And fear and hate, but love oh love
Abune and over aa.

His was a serious approach to marriage, but he was not always to
view the relationships of others in such light. Nicoll also tells of a
young man, who having spent all his savings on his lass at the
market saw her then unconcernedly take up with another. Upon
this sight he vainly tried to drown himself, but ultimately obtained
comfort by telling it 'an to his mither'.

Since Robert Nicoll's early teens he had suffered from chest
illnesses, and the harsh life on the farm and sleeping on a
makeshift hammock above his shop had taken their toll. By the
age of twenty-two he had secured the editorship of the *Leeds
Times*, a radical newspaper with a circulation of around 2,000.
Within a year he had built circulation up to 3,000, but at the
expense of his already fragile health.

Nicoll's lingering consumption began to develop dangerously
around this time and he was brought north to the house of a
friend in Edinburgh for rest, recuperation, and it was hoped, full
recovery. But Nicoll himself knew that this was to be his final
illness, and his only regret at the end was that he had not been able

to return to Tullybelton and the area of his childhood. His parents, alerted to their son's state on the afternoon of 6 December 1837, left home and walked overnight and half the next day the fifty-one miles to be with him. They arrived, exhausted, to see their son, about whom so many high hopes had been raised, die before nightfall on 7 December 1837.

The 1838 Statistical Account recorded that 'this was a young man of great promise cut off in the bloom of his life'. Editions of Nicoll's poetry followed each other in rapid succession after his death, in 1842, 1852, 1855 and 1877 until the centenary edition. Many of these volumes were subsequently reprinted. His work was also kept alive by John Wilson, a Perth lad whose equally remarkable life culminated in worldwide success as an opera singer, and who was an enthusiast for Scots poetry and song. Contemporary programmes demonstrate that he placed Nicoll's poetry firmly on a par with that of Rabbie Burns.

A grand centenary dinner was held in Nicoll's honour in Bankfoot in 1914. A contemporary account relates:

> Nothing like it had ever been seen in Bankfoot. So numerous were the applications for tickets that the original venue, the Village Hall, had to be abandoned in favour of the public hall and even that handsome and commodious apartment was hardly large enough to seat the company which numbered 150, of which 40 were ladies.

Perth provosts, past and present, attended as well as landowners and worthies from Bankfoot, and anyone who could remotely claim to possess kinship connections with the Nicoll family. Even the local aristocracy were out in force, a far cry from the days of Lady Nairne.

The dinner had come about as a result of a request by Nicoll's only surviving sister, by then a very old lady living in New Zealand. She had asked her neighbour Mr Kay, who was going to visit Scotland, to place a wreath on Nicoll's memorial. This direct news from the remaining family in New Zealand, and Kay's meeting with the Sprunt family of the area, who had been prime movers in the erection of the Nicoll memorial thirty years after his death and who had undertaken its maintenance, spurred the

Bankfoot community into action. The splendid dinner the community organised was a fitting commemoration of this short but fruitful life.

Nicoll's political writings also outlasted him. In 1920 Claudius Clear, alias Sir William Robertson Nicoll, wrote for the *British Weekly* an appreciation of the poet's radical views and outstanding editorship of the *Leeds Times*, comparing him favourably with Kennedy Jones, a founder of the *Daily Mail*, noting their similar strong qualities although remarking that 'between the consumptive Radical [Nicoll] who died at 23 and the prosperous Mr Kennedy Jones a great gulf is fixed', meaning that the gulf between the two was one of financial security.

However, Nicoll's posthumous reputation has declined and he is little known – and less studied – now, even around the area of his birthplace. Nothing in Bankfoot honours him. No sign indicates the presence of his obelisk above Tullybelton Farm. Perhaps it should be signposted from the A9. After all, as was said at the dinner in his honour 100 years after his birth: 'From herd laddie to editor's chair in 22 years is a feat even for Scotland.'

The Robert Nicoll obelisk is above Tullybelton Farm. Take the A9 for five miles north from Perth and follow signs to the west for Tullybelton, which is around four miles further on. The obelisk can be seen clearly from some miles distant, and is situated in a field just a hundred yards north of the farm.

Doocots from the dawn of time

The remains of doocots litter the countryside. Almost all are totally abandoned nowadays. They can be seen in the centre of fields or occasionally close by a road. Many can still be recognised by a muddle of fallen thick slate-like stones which formed the nesting boxes. Other clues are their position; they are almost always facing south, are usually in a field and close to a large house, or the remains of one. That puzzling sixteen-foot square building, which looks too small to have been a dwelling and which is almost totally derelict, is probably all that is left of a custom-built, stone-and-mortar breeding box for pigeons, a widespread adjunct to farming which lasted for hundreds of years.

Circular doocots like this one at the Melville roundabout on the A91, near Auchtermuchty, Fife, are one of the earliest types.

The earliest doocots were round, and as many of these are preserved by the various independent preservation societies around Scotland, they can be quite easily seen. Good examples are at Phantassie in East Lothian, Bogward by St Andrews and Gordonstoun on the Moray coast near Elgin.

The later style was a square structure of the 'lectern' shape, and the one at Finavon, on the A90 four miles north of Forfar, is open to the public. This lectern shape is the one most commonly seen today. But there are also more intriguing shapes. There is one at Glamis, Tayside, with a soaring pyramid as part of the rear wall. The doocot at Edzell in Angus looks like a miniature castle. Rothiemay, overlooking the River Deveron, is a classical structure

This double doocot built in the 'lectern' shape stands at Finavon, 4 miles north of Forfar beside the A90, and has been restored. One side currently houses pigeons.

akin to a chapel. Lesmurdie House in Moray is an ornamental lofty building of octagonal stone.

Doocots are known to have been in use in ancient Egypt and by the Romans. The latter fattened birds in a manner which gives a glimpse of the customs of the late Roman Empire: they were given white bread already half-chewed by men specially employed for the task. At the Bronze Age settlements of Skara Brae, Orkney, holes have been found which are very suggestive of pigeons' nests, and at Wemyss in Fife, pigeon holes were built into a cave which was then turned into a primitive doocot.

Early Hebrews too poor to sacrifice lambs were permitted to substitute doves, and pigeon droppings from doocots in Iran provided fertiliser for the successful cultivation of melon crops. The organised rearing of pigeons by keeping them in doocots was probably first introduced to Scotland by the Norman courtiers of Queen Margaret, and although Fife is one of the areas richest in doocots, Angus has over sixty still surviving. About twenty-five remain in Moray, six or so in Caithness and a few more in Orkney and Shetland.

The most obvious reason for pigeon-farming was to supply fresh meat throughout the winter as an alternative to salted meat.

Until the beginning of the eighteenth century, farmers slaughtered all but a few of their cattle at the beginning of the winter. Since it was impossible to feed the whole herd over the winter months, they kept just a few for breeding. As pigeons mate for life and reproduce themselves enthusiastically from spring to autumn, the monotonous diet could be relieved by catching the young fledgling birds ('peesers' in Scots) while they sat on the nest in the doocot box. Later, by shuttering or netting the pigeon holes to prevent escape, the older birds too were trapped for the table.

Towards the end of the eighteenth century, the introduction of the turnip or mangel-wurzel crop revolutionised farming by enabling the farmer to grow sufficient winter food for the herd. Thereafter more cattle could be kept alive over the winter and cattle could then be slaughtered for food all the year round. The heyday of the doocot was over. But farming traditions and superstitions die hard and a few ornamental boxes would continue to be built inside the tower which graced the top of the central part of many nineteenth-century symmetrical farm buildings. As late as 1850, Henry Stephens was writing in his comprehensive *Book of the Farm* that:

> A pigeon house is a necessary structure and may be made to contribute a regular supply of one of the best luxuries raised on a farm. As pigeons are fond of heat at all seasons, a room in the gable, above the bulls' hammels would suit well.

Wonderfully elegant examples of these towers can be seen at Stracathro, Pearsie and Woodmill Farms, all in Perthshire and Angus. At Stracathro, the doocot is built into the top of an octagonal tower, the pigeon entrances being placed above blocked arched recesses in each wall. These were once apparently filled with imitation window panes brushed with gold paint.

At least a hundred years prior to this time, however, every gentleman, feuar, and substantial farmer in Scotland was burdened with his 'puckle of land, a lump o' debt, a doocot and a law plea'. In addition, ecclesiastical establishments large and small also had their doocots, for example Crossraguel Abbey in Ayrshire, as well the parish minister with his more modest doocot at the bottom of the glebe garden.

At the other end of the social scale, the poor cottar too would have his couple of pigeons' nests in the gable wall, or in a wooden frame known as a fuie.

Most doocots were situated several hundred yards from the house and contained an average of several hundred nesting boxes. The problem these pigeon flocks caused to laird and crofter alike was their tendency to descend on grain fields and, at worst, decimate them. The laird was under no obligation to feed his birds and rarely did; his large flocks did not differentiate between his land and his neighbours'. Yet destroying another's birds was a severely punishable offence.

In 1617 an Act was passed in Scotland restricting the building of doocots to within two miles of those owning land whose annual value was ten chalders of grain (a chalder is a Scottish dry measure containing 16 bolls, a boll being about 68 kilos). In some parts of the country, little notice was taken of this edict.

In France, doocots were much larger and the swarms of pigeons which descended on the peasants' meagre crops was one of the goading influences in sparking off the French Revolution.

The shelter for the pigeons was provided by the structure itself, often tucked into the hillside and invariably facing south. (Only one example of a west-facing doocot is well known, at Pitscandy, Angus.) Small windows, generally high up in the gable walls gave ventilation, and protection from vermin was provided by deep stone ledges built into the wall, sometimes even two or three deep, running parallel to each other horizontally round the string-course. This ledge was called a strong-course, or rat-course, and prevented rats running up the walls and attacking the birds.

Nesting boxes lined the walls of the building. In the early days they were generally built from rough stone slabs with vertical divisions of rough stones. Later boxes were notable for being of beautifully dressed stone, or neat constructions of bricks or wood.

Why do so many doocots survive, if not intact then at least in a remarkably good state of repair, when the mansion houses for which they were constructed have long since gone? As the mansion house was replaced by a more modern version, the old house fell down or was de-roofed to avoid payment of roof taxes.

There was no roof tax on the doocot, so little could be saved in tax by demolishing its roof. Moreover doocots were functional buildings whose use did not diminish with changing styles of architecture.

Superstitions may have played their part too. Legend had it that to build a doocot meant the death within the year of the builder – the moral here being surely to keep one's existing cote in a healthy condition. Legend also had it that if the doocot fell ruinous, the laird's wife would meet her end within the year.

From a more practical point of view, doocots were often squat structures with massive thick walls, adapted to various uses – this would have aided their survival. At Lunan, Angus, for instance, the lower half of the doocot is big enough to house a small stable, the pigeon department being upstairs. Later, the lower half was used as the gardeners' toilet.

The earliest type of doocot was shaped like an old round beehive, and these date from the sixteenth century. The next development was a round structure with a pitched and slated roof, and the predominant style from the late sixteenth and seventeenth centuries was the 'lectern' shape. These usually incorporated a high wall on the north side and the roof slopes from there to the lower south wall. The gables are higher than the roof and thus make the roof a sheltered zone for the pigeons to sun themselves. Access for pigeons was through dormer windows in the roof, front or gable walls. This 'lectern' lean-to style was copied from the French dovecotes of the period, a legacy of the Auld Alliance. In southern France, it was necessary to preserve the pigeons from the mistral's fierce blast and this method of building proved suitable for the windswept zones of eastern Scotland too.

A desire to ornament doocots was evident. One senses a touch of one-upmanship; after all, people have always wanted to make grander buildings than their neighbours. Another reason for ornamentation could be that doocots were frequently visible not only from the house, but also to passers-by, so were designed to impress both social equals and the lesser orders. Even thrifty, hard-pressed farmers went in for splendid doocots.

Nesting boxes were often of dressed stone and made to a high standard of workmanship. Most doocots have nesting boxes starting at about one metre above ground level. Pigeons dislike nesting too close to the ground and have to be protected against vermin. Given a choice, pigeons will nest high, and this observation dictated the shape of the doocot.

Despite the heavy penalties for stealing pigeons, little was left to chance, and double doors were the order of the day. This also enabled the pigeon-catcher to shutter or net the pigeon entrances and stop the birds escaping through the doors. The peesers were caught on their nests and eggs were collected by ladder and also with a device called a potence, from a French word meaning gallows.

A central pole, rather like a telephone pole, was fixed between the floor and the ceiling of the doocot. The pole had struts on one side, so it looked rather like a very wide ladder clamped to the central pole. The whole contraption swivelled around. The collector of eggs or young birds would climb up the ladders, pushing himself with a foot against one side of the wall in order to manoeuvre round. A potence still exists at Fothringham, Angus. Pigeons are shy creatures and fly away at the least provocation, so catching the young and collecting eggs was frequently done at night, which must have been an eerie experience. By the time pigeon-farming declined, the methods of keeping them had advanced to a mechanically sophisticated level of efficiency. The doocots topping nineteenth-century farm buildings were surely a nostalgic afterthought. Indeed this can have been the only reason for the building of a free-standing one at Fornethy House, Glenisla, Angus, by the Misses Coats as late as 1915.

But perhaps the whole experience of fluttering doves is still treasured. Look at the new, ornamental doocots which abound.

Many doocots can be seen from a distance but two the public can see at close range are at: Finavon, Angus, four miles north of Forfar on the A90 and clearly visible from the road; and Melville doocot, Fife, a round-house near Auchtermuchty on the A91, just to the west of the junction with the A92.

Tales of tatties

They sport uncommon names, such as Queen Mary, Black and Blue Skerrie, Champion, Rocks, Shetland Black and Shetland Red, Katie Glover, Fortyfold and Edzell Blue. They are all varieties of potato, and each of these, along with a couple of hundred more varieties, can still be found in Scotland – although visitors to the local supermarket will never find most of them. Most of these potatoes with exotic names have over the years been superseded by more disease-resistant, heavier-cropping, less indented 'eye' tubers. But many of the old ones still beat the newer varieties in terms of taste.

Champion is dated from about 1876, and was commonly eaten as part of the staple diet of tattie and salt herring on the west coast of Scotland, where it continued to be grown long after it fell out of use in the rest of the country. Rocks is a very old main crop variety. Edzell Blue is a smallish cropper with regal purple skins and is still obtainable. Shetland Black is indeed almost black-skinned, although no one seems to know why or how this has occurred. Shetland Red could be a sea-faring arrival; the story goes that these red-skinned potatoes were grown from tubers washed ashore from a shipwreck. Katie Glover is a very old lady, having been named after the Fair Maid of Perth. Fortyfold sounds as though it was a bonus arrival and heavy cropper but is unlikely to be found today; it was scientifically dated in 1836, so was certainly older than this.

At the turn of the last century, the 116 acres of Mairsland Farm, just to the north of Auchtermuchty, Fife, was one of the most famous farms in Scotland for potatoes. Archibald Findlay was described by the *Scottish Farmer* at the time as being 'fairly entitled to the distinguished honour of being the Prince of potato rearers in the whole world'.

Archibald Findlay had many claims to fame. He bred Majestic and Eldorado, and for the first stock crop of the latter he turned down an offer of £200,000. He was a successful and innovative breeder of potatoes, always trying out new varieties on his family. He would bring a small bagful into the kitchen to be cooked for dinner, joking with the family that they were eating £50 worth of potatoes. And he would claim that his tatties played a part in winning the First World War, maintaining that 98% of the tatties fed to the troops between 1914 and 1919 were of his breeding, or derived from his potatoes.

Mairsland Farm is off the B936, a mile north of Auchtermuchty, Fife.

Rabbit food

Rabbits have for centuries been a source of food in Scotland, but although there are few accounts of the deliberate farming of rabbits for profit, there is one honourable exception.

An agricultural report of 1876 reported that the whole of the 700-acre island of Little Cumbrae was given over to rabbits, yielding a rent of £280 per annum. Around 300 to 500 dozen rabbits were killed there per year. The owner of the island was the Earl of Eglinton, the mastermind behind the Eglinton tournament. There seems to be no further account of the profitability of this venture, but perhaps it went the way of the tournament and was quietly abandoned.

The island of Little Cumbrae lies in the Firth of Clyde, between the southernmost tip of the island of Bute and Ayrshire.

Fife Tay sparling fishing

You can smell them in the water. It's just like cucumbers. If you're fishing the Tay, and you catch them with other fish, then the whole netful will smell of cucumber.

It's the last river where you can fish for them commercially, although I hear that it is still done on the Solway. At the turn of the century there used to be forty boats here in Newburgh. My boat, the *Fait*, is one of the last pair. It's the oldest boat afloat around here still being used.

So said Charlie Johnston, a fisherman most of his life, when well over retirement age.

Sparling (*Osmerus eperlanus*) belong to the family which includes more familiar species such as salmon, trout, char, whitefish and grayling. When fully grown they are around twelve to fourteen inches long, but the ideal length for selling is ten inches. They are like young herring in appearance, silvery in colour, but with a deeper belly. They are delicious to eat, and have a unique and distinctive flavour of clean, fresh cucumber.

Prized from the turn of the last century until just after the Second World War, they were considered a great delicacy and

One of the very last of the sparling boats, here moored at Newburgh in Fife. Now sunk, this boat was a final link with the traditional method of catching the small, silvery sparling in the lower reaches of the Tay.

Once a common dish for locals and a prized cash catch for hardworking fishermen before the Second World War, local children from Newburgh gaze at what is now a rare sight – adult sparling, which smell of cucumbers and used to be a great delicacy.

could command high prices. For such an unusual and highly prized fish, sparlings are famed only for their lack of fame.

Dr Clement Bruce Gunn, an assistant GP in Newburgh, Fife, in the 1880s, relates his views of the local gastronomic delights in his classic account of country medicine, *Leaves from the Life of a Country Doctor*:

> three local dispensations of Providence, at this epoch, afforded signal delight to a city bred boy like myself, who had seldom seem and never lived in the country. These were the pears (the juicy Bon Cretian variety which had been introduced by the French Benedictine monks to Lindores Abbey in the 12th century from Picardie, close to Paris), the salmon and the sparlings.
>
> Lastly to complete this gastronomic paradise ... the sparlings were in excellent condition just when the salmon season closed. They were packed into flat boxes as soon as caught and like the salmon, hurried off by special train to the London Market.

'They were a luxury fish', recalled the late Charlie Johnston, 'and at the turn of the century a box one foot wide, and just one fish deep went for 2s. 3d.' His friend and fellow fisherman, the late Lou Aitken, added,

> One time we had only smaller fish to send, so we just packed them up and sent them. We were paid exactly the same price.
>
> Then after the war, the demand started to fall off. The only reason I can think of is that the fat ration was cut, and as they used to be mainly shallow fried, that made cooking difficult. Billingsgate used to be a big market for us in the old days. Liverpool was the best, and there used to be a demand in the Netherlands, with Dutch boats coming over specifically to fish for them.

Few in Scotland would recognise sparling today. Charlie took a box over with him to a Fife coastal port, Anstruther, a bare twenty-five miles distant, to find that the fishermen there had neither heard of them nor recognised them.

In the 1980s, Dr Peter Maitland of the Stirling-based Fish Conservation Centre spent time studying their life cycle. There used to be a sparling population in the Forth, but it disappeared in the 1960s for unknown reasons, and certainly some swim around the Solway, though not in large enough quantities to support commercial fishing. Despite the fact that there seem to be only two populations of sparling left, one on either side of Scotland, the two colonies remain remarkably similar. It is almost impossible that they ever meet and interbreed. They spawn in fresh water and go down towards the sea to grow, returning again to spawn upriver. Most fish are caught well inland and upriver. Pollution might have decimated the population – Lou Aitken offered his view that 'the Forth was that manky, that even the flounders used to come to the surface for oxygen'.

Aside from being fished, sparling have several natural predators in the wild, such as other fish and birds, and they themselves eat a wide variety of crustaceans and small fish. They are also cannibals and will happily eat smaller sparling.

To catch them, the nets are thrown out from the sides of the boat. The mesh is tapered like a windsock on two booms, the top one is made from a wooden beam, the bottom one made of iron. The boat sits in a likely place for scooping up the sparling with these great batwing nets slung out on either side. Sparling are caught about an hour before the tide ebbs and again an hour after the tide turns. The fish seem to be just drifting in the water and it is the tide ebbing and flowing which pushes them into the nets. It is very hard work, and discouraging for newcomers to try.

Local fishermen described how they caught them best in muddy water, when the net is rendered invisible. If a high tide disturbed the mud, then you made a catch. When there was a frost, with clear water, there was no such luck. The nets get heavy with mud and silt. As for the strange shape of these nets, it was a design which was improved by default and a measure of industrial espionage. Lou Aitken's father had found himself eavesdropping on an interesting conversation in one of the local pubs. Several English boats had appeared and fished very successfully for sparling in the river. Lou overheard a description of just how these fishermen had crafted the special shape of their nets, and simply went home and copied it. His catches then improved dramatically.

8

The sea, ships and watery yarns

Loch Ewe and the Russian convoys

Despite its beauty, a sense of isolation is strong at the edge of Loch Ewe, once picked as an excellent hiding place for assembling ships before they set off on the North Atlantic convoys in the Second World War.

The generation which saw the loch 'black with ships' and maintained that you could almost walk across on their decks without getting your feet wet is nearly gone now, but the remains can still clearly be seen. The coastal defence artillery sites, with their gun emplacements and concrete command posts, are still there, in a commanding position on the cliff tops. Close by is evidence of peat cutting, carried out by the gunners to obtain some much needed fuel to keep them warm during the long cold nights. At Black Bay the remains of two lifeboats from the *USS William Welch* can also just about be detected. It is poignant indeed to stand alongside the memorial to the dead at Cove, and realise this was an area where many sailors, drawn from all over the UK and beyond, all too often had their last sight of land.

Cove is at the end of the B8057 about ten miles north of the junction at Poolewe with the A832.

Coves for cunning U-boats

Not all the hiding places for ships on the west coast were the prerogative of the Allies in either of the world wars. In remote areas, the possibility of a snatched sheep or two for dinner and a few snatched days of relative calm and safety was a great attraction, for the German military forces at least.

Few of the owners of the many yachts moored in one of the most popular havens for pleasure boats, at Ardfern in Loch Craignish, can suspect that the largest island in the centre of the loch, Eilean Righ, provided food and sanctuary for at least one German U-boat.

Forsyth Hamilton, who for many years had a fish-smoking business in the Ardrishaig area, recalled the following tale.

A friend of his was in Iran many years after the war, and at an official dinner sat next to an elderly German, who enquired from where in Scotland he hailed. The Scot, who came from Argyll, was intrigued, and asked him why he wanted to know. Gradually it transpired that his dinner neighbour had been a U-boat commander in the First World War, and strayed into Craignish. One of his officers was landed and managed to kill three sheep which they then had to drag back. Here their difficulties started. Catching and killing the sheep was easy compared with manoeuvring the carcasses up onto the deck of the submarine and then down the conning tower. However, such succulent fresh supplies were not going to be abandoned, and finally not only did they stuff the entire booty into the submarine, they butchered them and, anxious not to waste a morsel, tied the tripe (stomach) to the conning tower to clean it. The smell was apparently appalling, but the former commander still remembered the meat as being the best mutton he had ever tasted. Although decades had elapsed, the commander was in for a sharp surprise. The Argyll man announced that those sheep had belonged to his cousin, who used the island for grazing, and therefore the German should pay him £30 for the sheep!

This was not the only tale of wartime acquisition of fresh meat. Clas Uig, an isolated cove on the island of Islay, was also an enemy submarine lair, and remained a secret until the story appeared in the October 1965 edition of *Scottish Field*. According to Rosemary Hamilton, the writer of the article entitled 'Hidden Harbour', a German visitor appeared in 1921 at the White Hart Inn in Port Ellen on the south coast of Islay and caused quite a sensation by announcing that he wished to see the view from the landward side of the place where he had holed up from time to time in his U-boat in the First World War. The cove which he found had a small pier made up of colossal stones and was known to have been used by cattle drovers two centuries ago. In his book *Laird of the Light Houses* John Rickman, who owned a lighthouse on Jura, tells how he became so intrigued by the story that he ventured down to see the coastal haven for himself. Clas Uig is situated close to the large Celtic cross of Kildalton, reputed to be the sole complete cross in Scotland, and, although finding this a magnificent sight, he could hardly wait to press on to the hidden cove. To reach the cove, which is on private land, they had to scramble along the shore via Port Mhor and Carraig Mhor. The quay is tucked away, and the tiny sheltered harbour provided a perfect secret haven for the U-boat crew to refresh their provisions, again claiming the odd sheep from the hill. It is touching that for someone caught up in war the memories were so special that the German returned to this place of solace. Had he not done so, the visits of the U-boat would have remained a secret forever.

Less secretive, and on a far greater scale, was the arrival of a fleet of five French frigates commanded by a Captain Thurot on 16 February 1760 in Aros Bay, but a couple of minutes' sail from Clas Uig. The frigates were to have supported Bonnie Prince Charlie in his attempt to claim his throne. They had already been holed up in their home harbours for months by the English fleet, but had finally broken through, sailing to Gothenburg, then Bergen, and then through the storms of the North Sea, losing one of their ships. By the time the fleet arrived off the coast of Islay, the remaining men of the original 1,200 land forces were starving. Contemporary accounts describe how the two local lairds, Archibald Macdonald and Godfrey Macneil, went out to see the ships, at first thinking they were British ships in distress. They must have had very mixed feelings when they discovered that they were French, no doubt supporting the Jacobite cause, but apprehensive of the danger in dealing with these foreigners. But pragmatism won the day. The men were anxious to obtain provisions and Macdonald and Macneil persuaded the local men to bring cattle, poultry and meal to sell.

From Campbell of Ardmore the French also obtained forty-eight bullocks and seventeen bags of oatmeal, though many of the 200 French sailors allowed ashore could wait no longer, and dug up potatoes and cabbages by hand, eating them raw. There was a little local difficulty when it appeared no payment might be forthcoming, but Thurot ordered his officers to settle up. It was a last supper for many, as he and many of his men were killed in a battle with the English ships *Eolus*, *Pallas* and *Brilliant* while making for France.

In contrast to the sheep-stealing and provisioning of both the French in the 1760s and the Germans in 1914–18, a far more terrifying ordeal took place in 1831 at the hands of Captain Duplait of the picturesquely named *True Blooded Yankey*, a privateer carrying 260 men and twenty-six guns which anchored at what is now named Port Charlotte. Spying the harbour packed with merchant ships, he rifled them of anything worth taking, estimated at a value of £600,000, and then set them on fire, making off across the Atlantic with his booty. Success, however, was short lived, as she was captured by a British ship shortly afterwards and carried down to the River Plate, where she ended her days. (William Macdonald, *Descriptive and Historical Sketches of Islay*, Glasgow, 1850.)

Loch Craignish is about twenty-five miles south of Oban on the A816.

Scooping out salmon

Still dotted along both banks of the Tay between Perth and Dundee is a series of isolated cottages. They are so close to the river's edge that it looks as though you could fish for your supper from the front window.

At first glance they appear to be identical cottages, but since many have no obvious road or path to them, and are at least a kilometre from a main road, it can be tricky to check this for certain. Some are ruinous, some relatively new, built at least since the last war. Some are well maintained, and obviously used, some are roofless, others are at a stage somewhere in between, complete with roofs, but gaping holes for windows. If you were to venture down across fields to peer inside, you would see that some of the ruinous ones still contain the remains of beds – all single, but frequently built in pairs, head to foot. If you were to look inside the well-maintained ones, you would see cookers as well as modern bunk beds in a similar arrangement.

Remains of such cottages are to be found not only up and down the Tay, but on coasts all round Scotland where salmon fishing was or still is a business. This is not fly-fishing though; it involves netting salmon as they swim upriver, and is the basis of a small industry which could well be in its death-throes. Many of the netting rights have been bought up by trusts whose interests lie in the preservation of the rod-fishing salmon rights further upstream.

The origins of many of these small fishing bothies are not well documented, having been of little importance in the records of the estates upon which they were built. But generally, the older, ruinous ones were probably built at the end of the nineteenth century. Others have been constructed in a fluctuating but continuous programme of building ever since. Close to some modern bothies down by the Tay can be found an original, earlier one, smothered in brambles and fairly ruinous, many of its stones having been used in the construction of the newer house.

Hauling in salmon on the River Tay with large nets changed little from medieval times right up to the twentieth century, and was a favourite seasonal occupation of students, whose energy was required for the hard physical work. All Tay netting rights have now ceased, and this photograph, taken in the 1980s, illustrates a lost industry.

Salmon packed within ice in the distinctive wooden boxes owned by Tay Salmon fisheries were rushed to Perth Station and sent on the overnight train to London.

Why these bothies were built in such isolated locations owes little to chance, but a great deal to the ability of the fishermen to launch nets from that location, and the success-rate of their catch. If the catch-rate over the years was good, then the bank was well built up so that the boats could be easily launched and the men could walk along the shore and haul in the salmon. When the bothy lapsed into a poor condition, and the catching was still good, then the salmon-fishing company would build another. If, on the other hand, the fishing deteriorated, then the bothy was unceremoniously abandoned, and fishing was taken further up or down stream. On the Tay, many abandoned elderly bothies can be seen on the south bank between Newburgh and Balmerino, and right along the north bank between Perth and Dundee. One of the last to be built, which was never really successful owing to the building of the Friarton Bridge almost overhead, can be seen just east of Perth, north of Junction 10 on the M90.

The size of the bothy depended on the length of time round the tides that the fishing could operate. If it was only a short time, fewer men were needed, and the bothy was correspondingly small, and the reverse for an area when the fishing could operate for many more hours round the high tide.

The bothies acquired the names which were given to the local piece of water. A glance at the Ordnance Survey map of the Tay between Perth and Dundee reveals some strange names. Why was 'The Langlaw' so named, for example? Apparently because it was the scene of an intractable dispute between two brothers who conducted endless lawsuits against each other, all because of the fishing rights, of course. These rights were valuable enough to be frequently contested. Then there are bothies called 'The Wonder', 'The Reekit Lady' and 'The Gutterhole' – this last meaning a devil of a place.

The boats which were used by salmon netters were built to a design unchanged since the sixteenth century. These cobles, still used on the great fishing rivers, are indeed still constructed and so well developed for their purpose that their design has shown no need for modern modifications apart from the addition of an engine to replace oars. When cobles sink, apparently they can be immediately righted, emptied out, and put straight back to use again. Their elegant shape belies their workhorse capabilities. The flat-back panel at the stern of the boat was used for the nets.

The manning of the salmon bothies was a seasonal affair. The season ran from the first week in February till the end of August, and the fishing hours were from 6 a.m. on Monday to 6 p.m. on Saturday. The men who worked in these bothies often came from generations of the same families, brothers, sons and fathers working together. After the fishing finished, there was other casual seasonal work to turn to, such as harvesting. The men would leave home on a Sunday night, carrying their food for the week, and wend their way down to their bothy. Once there they stuck to a system of five hours working, seven hours off. Most bothies had at least one or two fireplaces, set into the gable-end walls, and they would be divided into at least two rooms. Often the centre section, opposite the front door, was an open space with open beams at least a couple of metres off the floor where clothes and boots could be dried. Later bothies had their fireplaces set into the inner walls of each room, the warmth from the flues spilling into this central area for drying clothes. Few, if any, of the older bothies had electricity, being in such an isolated position, and this was true even of bothies in use well into the twentieth century.

Before their recent demise, the fishing bothies had become more civilised, cooking facilities better, but the method of net fishing for salmon, still occasionally carried out on the coast, has changed hardly at all. The net is piled onto the boat, the boat sweeps out in an arc, the other shore-based fisherman dragging his end of the net along the shore, in line with the boat. The two ends are then winched together, the fish being trapped in the net bag which is created. The fish are dispatched, weighed and put into the cold store. In the old days, the fish would be collected each day by a boat going up and down the river and taken to a central point where they would be kept in an ice house, and sent off to the market by train. By the end of their lives in the 1990s, the bothies had vehicle access and the fish was collected by road.

Fishing bothies can still be seen on the north bank of the Tay four or five miles east of Perth.

Tides, rocks and cutting devices

In 1782 a gentleman named Francis Douglas observed that 'one of our kings gave to the town of Crail three mills', and that they were situated 'a few miles to the north where they are still called the King's Mills'. By the end of the eighteenth century the burgh community only possessed two of these common mills, and one of them was 'turned by salt water admitted during the flood tide into a reservoir and discharged upon the wheel after the tide had ebbed'.

A tide mill was an innovative and surprisingly simple way of harnessing the power of the sea. The more usual mill wheel was positioned vertically and the paddles were driven by rushing water channelled down a mill lade, which was usually a man-made cutting, fed by water stored upstream in a man-made reservoir, or connected to a loch which held a constant and reliable amount of water. A tide mill was placed horizontally in an enlarged natural opening in rocks, using the incoming water as power. A man-made dam was built in the rocks and the water from the incoming tide was trapped in this pond by a sluice, and then released to supply power as the tide went out.

The tide mill which is still to be clearly seen at Fife Ness north of Crail is probably the one mentioned in the Statistical Account of 1793 by Francis Douglas. The use made of the tide mill does not seem to be recorded, but there was another one at Burntisland, which is further south and west round the Fife coastline.

Less than a hundred metres from the tide mill, on the opposite side of the road, is a small cottage. Opposite this cottage on the edge of the rocks, and above the high-tide mark, is another curious indentation, although this was gouged out for quite a different reason.

On the flat rocky shore, but a couple of metres from the road, are two concentric grooved circles. The circles are about two to three metres in diameter and look as though they have been made with a giant pair of compasses. In the centre of this circle is a hole.

These concentric circles, cut into the rocks just at the high-water mark at Fife Ness, were originally thought to be the site of a gun emplacement. In fact they are the template for cutting the stones for the Carr Beacon Lighthouse.

The truth is far more intriguing, as it was from this foreshore that the Carr Rock Beacon was shipped out, stone by stone, to be constructed between 1812 and 1821, when the first warning marker ever to be built on that treacherous rock was finally completed. The concentric circles were used as the template to cut the stones needed for the circular base of the beacon.

The beacon was in fact an open-work cast-iron ball on cast-iron legs, warning shipping of the navigational hazard. There was no actual illumination, although it was once intended to have a bell set atop the tower. It was to have been rung by an intricate method using the rising and falling tides, on the same principle as the workings of a grandfather clock. The tide rushing through a small gap at the base, below the water level, would push up the lower drum within the central tower, as seen in the original design. This would wind up the cog wheel in the larger chamber as it rose each time, and when the tide rushed out, the lower drum would fall again, bringing the cog wheel into reverse. The cog wheel would tug on the bell at the top and this would sound a warning.

It appears that the bell idea was abandoned very late in the construction as the need to finish the beacon became pressing. Engineer Robert Stevenson had made a model of this bell apparatus and had it working for six months, but he finally conceded that with the difficulties he had already encountered and the extra cost involved, a simple marker was all that he could produce.

There are few, if any, working sites left where there is evidence of how lighthouses or beacons were constructed, making Fife Ness a fascinating link with the ingenuity and bravery of Robert Stevenson and his builders.

A warning light was long overdue on the Bell Rock, another hazard standing further out to sea than the Carr, as in 1799 alone an astonishing seventy ships were wrecked on this jagged reef, 370 yards long and just over 100 yards broad. The water surrounding it is shallow, and the rock itself is visible only at low tide, when the tips of the crags rise six feet above the sea.

So treacherous to shipping were the Bell and Carr rocks, situated as they are between the shipping routes to the Forth and the Tay, and so frequent were the wrecks there, local legend states that the farmers who had lands adjacent to the shore area could command higher prices for their ground than further inland. The reason was simple. The quality of the land was no better but added value came from the loot washed ashore, and the farmer who lived closest managed to run down faster and claim the goodies first. Perhaps there is a grain of truth in tales of farmers staggering around drunk on the fine clarets and cognacs before flexing their carpentry skills on new pig sties with the best cedar, and fencing their land with teak and mahogany.

The number of shipwrecks, however, forced the Commissioners for Lighthouses to take action. It was not that there was a reluctance to see a light erected upon, firstly, the Bell Rock, it was simply that the task seemed impossible. Stevenson was the man to tackle the seemingly impossible. As the Bell Rock light shone out for the first time on 1 February 1811, the Commissioners resolved to tackle the Carr Rock.

Stevenson at first decided that a masonry tower should be erected, and what is more, he could do this from the shore at Fife Ness. On anything but a flat calm day, today's visitors to this shingle beach with its sharp jagged rocks running out to generally a choppy sea, will marvel that anyone would choose this spot for any building project, let alone one which was ambitious and untested.

In order to improve the location as a place from which to land the quarried stone, transport it up the beach, cut it into the exact shape and reload it onto boats for the trip out to the Carr Rock, the sheltering harbour had to be improved. Great slabs of stone formed the harbour wall, but only very careful scrutiny will reveal any remains now. A tub-way, or tram track, was laid for the transportation of stone to and from the unloading place on the quay to the spot where the stone was cut at the rock template. The sandstone for the beacon came from the quarry near the mouth of the Pitmilly Burn on land belonging to Lord Kellie, near Boarhills about four miles to the north of Fife Ness. The concentric grooves measured out the accurate circumference of the stones, and each stone was then cut and shaped to fit into its neighbour just as the pieces of wood or card are cut to make a jigsaw. This gave the structure the greatest strength.

While not so large a project as the construction of the Bell Rock Lighthouse, which took four years, the building of the Carr Beacon was to present similar problems. But perhaps even Stevenson was unaware of the superhuman efforts required.

The rock itself, a mile from the shore, is a tide-covered reef, and try as they might, it was impossible to detect a base more than eighteen feet in diameter, and sections of this were below the water level even at the lowest of low tides. At least sixteen ships had foundered there before a buoy was successfully placed in 1809. Not that the buoy was reliable: Stevenson observed, perhaps with a tinge of nervousness, that 'though inspected regularly and replaced, the buoy broke loose five times in four years'.

The problem was the continual rubbing of the mooring against the sandstone bottom, which acted as a giant sheet of sandpaper, an ominous prediction of future problems. In order to lay the foundations, coffer dams had to be put in place and removed again after each working day. These are vertical tube-like constructions – wooden in this case – placed on the sea bottom to allow work to be carried out below water level.

In 1812, Stevenson began, but managed just forty-one hours of work during the entire first year, owing to the weather and almost insurmountable trials of attempting to build foundations virtually underwater. Next year was a little better, and fifty-three hours were logged. In 1815, just as nine stones for the third layer were in place, the sea took her revenge and most were swept off and out to sea. A lesser man might have been daunted, perhaps likely to cast himself off the remaining blocks. Stevenson merely analysed the situation, commenting that the gale from the east which blew up on 3 October must have annihilated the cement before it had time to harden, although he was using the same tried and tested methods of dovetailing as he had used for the Bell Rock.

Indomitably – or perhaps because neither Stevenson nor the commissioners had any alternative – they pressed on the following year, and built the structure up to twenty feet, about half the projected height. Now Stevenson lowered down four tons of lead, all transported out in rowing boats, to help stabilise and strengthen the lower chamber, and by 1817 the masonry was complete. In five heroic summers they had managed to build what had seemed impossible, a thirty-four-course masonry tower. But within a few months, only five courses remained, the others beaten down by the November gales.

However, Stevenson was unbeaten. He planned and built six cast-iron columns to the remainder of the masonry, a tripod which supported a caged dome, on top of which was a circular beacon. After six years of desperately harsh working conditions in open boats, and at a total cost of around £5,000, the warning to shipping was in place.

The original structure eventually rusted away and has been replaced twice, most recently with a simple pole carrying a radar reflector – efficient and safe, and a memorial to awesome human endeavour.

Fife Ness, Fife, is on a secondary road about a couple of miles north-east of Crail. Follow this road out of Crail towards Fife Ness, passing the many remains of the old RAF station to right and left of the road. Eventually the road ends at the golf club. Just before you reach the golf club there is a road to the right signposted to the coastguard station at Fife Ness. Turn right onto this road and as it drops down to a dip, round a corner and into another small bay with a small cottage on the right, pull off the road by the beach and walk back northwards to the first small bay. Down on the rocks there is a distinct inlet with a rectangular 'dam' cut out of the rocks. The remains of the cutting jig can be seen only a couple of metres into the rock, opposite the small cottage and a little to the north. Signposts point to the mill and cutting-jig area.

Lord Ullin's daughter

When James Boswell and Dr Samuel Johnson reached the ferry crossing from Mull to Ulva in 1773 on their tour of the Hebrides, Boswell recorded that there was a pause in their progress upon discovering that there was no boat.

> We should have been in a very bad situation, had there not fortunately been lying in the little sound of Ulva an Irish vessel, the *Bonnetta* of Londonderry, Captain McLure, the master. He himself was at McQuarrie's; but his men obligingly came with their long-boat and ferried us over.

A familiar poem to generations of Scots children by nineteenth-century Glasgow poet Thomas Campbell tells of the loss at sea of Lord Ullin's daughter as she tried to elope. This cross, at Oskamull, inscribed with the poem, commemorates her death.

The little harbour at which they probably landed is still there, tucked away in a quiet, sheltered cove, and directly opposite is the site supposedly holding the grave of a daughter, immortalised many years after her death by a tutor at Calgary, a small village on the north-west coast of Mull (after which the large city of Calgary in Canada was named).

The tutor was Thomas Campbell, and the subject of his poem was a daughter of Sir Allan McLean of Knock, 'Lord Ullin's Daughter', who was trying to elope with a son of the chief of Ulva. Boswell and Johnson chose to cross the straits to Ulva from

Gribun, passing by Inch Kenneth Island, described by Boswell as 'a pretty little island, about a mile long and about half a mile broad'. Here they were introduced to a later Sir Allan Maclean, the chief of his clan, and they also met his two young daughters.

The probable grave of Lord Ullin's daughter is apparently close to where her body was washed up, and is now commemorated by a splendid cross and inscribed with the entire poem.

Thomas Campbell (1777–1844) was the son of a Glasgow merchant and one of the founders of the University of London. He was very popular in his day as the writer of stirring poems and ballads, of which 'Lord Ullin's Daughter' is one of the best remembered. The poem begins:

> *A Chieftain to the Highlands bound*
> *Cries 'Boatman, do not tarry!*
> *And I'll give thee a silver pound*
> *To row us o'er the ferry!'*
>
> *'Now who be ye, would cross Lochgyle,*
> *This dark and stormy water?'*
> *'O I'm the chief of Ulva's Isle,*
> *And this, Lord Ullin's daughter.*
>
> *'And fast before her father's men*
> *Three days we've fled together,*
> *For should he find us in the glen,*
> *My blood would stain the heather.*
>
> *'His horsemen hard behind us ride –*
> *Should they our steps discover,*
> *Then who will cheer my bonny bride,*
> *When they have slain her lover?'*

Alas! The hapless pair chose a treacherous crossing of the loch in stormy weather and perished.

Isle of Mull. To find the cross commemorating Lord Ullin's daughter, take the B8073 on the west side of Mull from Gruline north-west. About half a mile short of the schoolhouse opposite the road to Ulva Ferry, there is a track almost opposite Oskamull down left to the shore. Follow this and the cross comes into view near the shore.

Roofed by a lifeboat

Stronsay was one of the busiest and largest herring harbours in the north. It is an island which relied for its livelihood on the sea, so it is only to be expected that boats have been put to more uses here than in the average small Scottish community. The upturned boat on the pier is, according to local writer Bill Vevers, often bypassed by tourists and ignored by the locals. But this upturned boat became the roof of a small house, complete with chimney and a door facing the road. She was used as a shed, to store creels and garden tools, and as a shelter for fishermen mending their nets. Her origins, however, had no connection at all with fishing or with Orkney.

She is, in fact, a sad relic of an unenviable encounter between a 14,000-ton liner and a U-boat, and holds the record of being part of the first ship to be torpedoed in the Second World War.

Wood was in such scarce supply in the islands of Shetland and Orkney that wooden boats which had become unseaworthy and not worth repairing were used as roofs for sheds and small houses. Many still stand on the islands to this day. This photograph was taken in Orkney in the early 1900s.

The upturned boat is one of the liner's lifeboats, which drifted ashore months later on a lonely Orkney beach where she was rescued and put to her new use.

The SS *Athenia*, on her way from Liverpool to Canada with 1418 passengers on board, was a sixteen-year-old Glasgow-based liner from the Donaldson Line. On board on the evening of Sunday 3 September 1939, Captain James Cook had been informing his passengers of the ship's immunity to attack from enemy submarines under international law. However, lifeboat drill was regularly practised as a precaution.

Bill Vevers described how U-boat 30, commanded by twenty-six-year-old Kapitanleutnant Fritz Julius Lemp, fired a salvo of torpedoes at the undefended ship just after 7.40 p.m. A nightmare situation immediately developed, as one of the torpedoes struck the *Athenia* on the port side and shattered the bulkhead between the boiler rooms, allowing water to flood into the damaged compartments. Passengers then found themselves trapped, as the explosion had wrecked the stairways to the upper decks where the lifeboats were.

Soon after this the U-boat surfaced with the intention of shooting down the *Athenia*'s wireless aerials to prevent her from transmitting warning signals. At this point the commander realised that he had hit a passenger ship, in violation of both international law and his own strict instructions. The submarine U-30 then submerged without attempting to offer the assistance demanded by international submarine protocol.

However, signals from the stricken ship had been received by distant Royal Navy destroyers and by merchant ships in the area, but it was the early hours before they reached the scene. The *Athenia*, surrounded by bobbing lifeboats, was still afloat. The Norwegian freighter *Krute Nelson* was first to arrive and immediately began to pick up survivors, although hampered by a heavy swell. One lifeboat held four crewmen and fifty-two women. As she came alongside the ship, she was drawn under the propeller. The bottom of the boat was ripped to pieces and only nine of those on board survived.

The US steamer *City of Fline* and the motor yacht *Southern Cross* joined the rescue and between them took off 1,300 survivors before the *Athenia* finally sank. The survivors were taken to Galway, Ireland, but 118 lives had been lost.

One empty lifeboat which drifted ashore was apparently later bought by Dennisons Shipowners, Shapinsay, where she lay at the pier for a while. But Davidson's seaweed factory was in operation in Stronsay at the time and they bought the boat and towed it back to Stronsay behind their motor boat, the *Char*.

Mrs Margaret Miller of Orkney lived on the island at the time and remembered this, as well as the workers nicknaming the boat Desperate Dan. Along with another boat, the *Mim*, it was used for collecting seaweed which was processed as meal at the local factory.

Later in the war, some of the workers were called up for military service and others had to leave the island. Both boats were then hauled up and the factory closed down and never reopened.

After the war, Jim Chalmers of Seafield bought the lifeboat, and took it up to his house at Bremners. Here he built a foundation of stone, on which he positioned the boat bottom-up and made her into a shed. A door, two windows and a brick-built chimney were added, a boiler inserted, and the building was used as a wash-house and coal-shed.

Mrs Miller remembers that it was very common to use boats as sheds. This was before the days of ready-to-construct wooden sheds, and wood was a scarce commodity on the islands. She casts her mind back to the 'boatie' houses which were adapted to house chickens, ducks and pigs as well as store coal and garden or fishing implements. Her father made a shed for coal by cutting a boat in half, building a shaped wall as a foundation. She remembers that it was finished off with a smart brass hook on the door.

The island of Stronsay is one of the islands north-east of the Orkney mainland. Whitehall is where the ferry lands from the mainland.

A very rare sailing reminder of a bygone age is also finishing her days as the roof of a garage on Foula, Shetland. This is only one of the three sixareens left in Shetland, the second being an altered version on Fetlar, while the third is safely in the Shetland Museum. However, there is a newly built sixareen to be seen on

Unst within the protecting corrugated sheeting of what looks like an old shed, but was built as the Swedish Mission to Seamen about 1910. This boat, along with several others, has been built or restored by Duncan Sandison, a native of Shetland and a boat enthusiast. Mr Sandison started his collection of old boats in 1972, when he realised that the old wooden boats were gradually disappearing from the beaches. He knew that unless he could rescue some examples and store them under cover, they would be lost forever.

The old Swedish Kirk had been used by the Swedish line fishermen who used to call at Baltasound in quite large numbers on their way to the fishing grounds west of Shetland. The Swedes have long gone and the building now just looks like a shed.

The Shetland sixareen was the most famous of all the Shetland boats. At the beginning of the nineteenth century it was estimated that between 400 and 500 boats and almost 3,000 men were engaged in fishing. The rebuilt sixareen is 9.15 metres long, but in earlier times, sixareens – so named because they were a six-oared boat – were smaller than this.

Mr Sandison's boat is called the *Far Haaf* and is named after the offshore fishing grounds on which this type of craft used to fish a century ago. The Far Haaf area was about forty miles offshore and in good weather the boats would stay at sea for at least a day and a night, or more, depending on the catch.

David Leask, who helps Duncan Sandison in the Boat Haven Project, explained that as the sixareen is an open boat, the sail would be used as shelter overnight, while the fishing lines which were strung out in the water acted as an anchor. On board would be a cast-iron kettle, which was heated on top of an iron basket filled with peat. A large flat stone would be placed in the foot of the boat and the basket would be placed on top of this.

A total of eight boats can be seen in the Unst Boat Haven Project, along with a collection of maritime artefacts, old photographs, and copies of documents relating to Shetland fishing.

Unst, Shetland. To find the Haven, come off the ferry at Baltasound and follow the Shore Road to the north side.

The *Far Haaf* is an example of a sixareen boat, used around the Shetland and Orkney islands and designed to go around 40 miles from shore. For overnight shelter, the sail would be taken down and used as a cover for the crew.

The kirk on the beach

The Free Church in the Isle of Whithorn rises just above the sea, poised at the water's edge like a squat, white-harled look-out building. Why is it located so precariously? Has the sea come closer since it was built in 1844? Was it not somewhat unwise to site this building so close to the sea, even in a sea-faring community?

Its date of 1844 gives the main clue to why it was so sited. In the aftermath of the Disruption, the Free Church decided to set up two congregations in the parish of Whithorn, but the laird of Glasserton owned all the available land, and being a staunch supporter of the Establishment, he refused to feu a site for the new Free Church.

Undeterred, the local civic fathers of the day found a loophole. The harbour was owned by the town, and a piece of ground just on the high-tide mark was cunningly earmarked for the site. So the church was built, and stands to this day as a memorial to the ingenuity and determination of the folk of the day. They laboured to build a church which has been baptised on a regular basis, twice a day on the high tide, for a century and a half, and which reminds today's worshippers of their hard-won building.

Isle of Whithorn, Dumfries and Galloway, is on the A746 about twenty miles south of Newton Stewart.

A far light

The lighthouse on the island of Scalpay in the Outer Hebrides must be high on the list of unusual holiday resorts, if not unique. Not that you camp out in the lighthouse tower itself. The accommodation is in the lighthouse keepers' cottages at the base of the tower. The light itself shines out nightly, but is now automated and no longer requires the care of lighthouse keepers.

The original lighthouse lens sits in splendour in the Royal Museum of Scotland in Edinburgh. Made in 1907 by Chance Brothers of Birmingham for the Northern Lighthouse Board, with a clockwork rotation motor by James Dove of Edinburgh, the lens itself weighs an incredible three tons. The great size of the glass prisms was necessary because they had to be able to withstand the tremendous heat from the light source without cracking. Most lenses, because of their huge weight and unwieldiness, were simply chucked into the sea at the end of their working life. It was the only practical option to take. This lens was dismantled and rebuilt. So whether holidaying in Harris, or musing in the museum, cast a thought to the making and then dismantling of such a mammoth piece of glass.

Close by this wonder in the Chambers Street museum in Edinburgh is another quaint piece of lighthouse construction, closely associated with lenses like the Harris one. This is the lantern housing which protected these valuable lenses. The lantern housing is a white-painted octagonal iron structure, rather like a conservatory or greenhouse minus its glass. The one in the museum must have originally contained a lens similar to the Scalpay one on exhibit close by, but was first used at Girdle Ness, near Aberdeen. All lighthouse lenses would have been protected by lantern housing such as this, but this is the only known surviving example. After having been installed at Girdle Ness in 1933, it was then updated and brought to Inchkeith in the Forth (an island which can be clearly seen from the road and rail bridges).

Lanterns such as this were designed and installed round the Scottish coasts by the Northern Lighthouse Board's first engineers, Thomas Smith (appointed in 1787), and Robert Stevenson (appointed in 1799). Placed high up at the tip of the lighthouses, which were built in the wildest and most exposed areas of the Scottish coasts, and more than likely never examined at close range by anyone other than the lighthouse men, the imaginative decoration on this lantern housing is astonishing.

Why would such intricate detail be applied to a structure which would never been seen? Simply a desire by the craftsmen to achieve a work of art to be rightly proud of. Perhaps there would have been superstition. Who knows.

The nine decorative castings round the lantern seem to be symbolic of the work of the Northern Lighthouse Board in making navigation safe round the hazardous coast of Scotland and the Isle of Man. Look closely and you will see the three-legged symbol of the Isle of Man. There is also a torch (the symbol of the Bishop's Rock), a lightship and a sea serpent. The decorative fish handles, complete with scales, are elegant and add another fascinating but understandable symbolic element to the lantern. But what is an Egyptian grave doing here, and an Indian symbol?

That the lantern housing ended up in the museum at all is matter of chance. In 1985 staff from the museum collected the redundant optic and foghorn from the island and spotted this housing lying to the side. They arranged its transport to the museum, where it can now be seen.

The island of Scalpay is just to the east of Harris in the Outer Hebrides. The lighthouse is on the eastern extremity, at the northern entrance to East Loch Tarbert.

Naval and military mysteries

The island of Eilean Choraidh is more or less in the centre of Loch Eriboll. This island was used by the Fleet Air Arm to rehearse the attack on the *Tirpitz* in Norway in 1944. There are few details of the precise use made of the loch by the Navy during and since the war. From time to time, convoys were seen and sheltered there and it has been used much by individual and small groups of ships. More recently an amphibious exercise took place in the vicinity three years after the Falklands War (1983) to assess the difficulties and lessons learned.

Above Portnancon, a pier about halfway down the west side of the loch, are stones set into the hillside. These spell out the names of some of the ships that have used the loch. The tradition seemingly began as sailors came ashore to the post office at Portnancon, and then would place the stones on the hillside, whitewashed for clarity.

It is thought that some ships put in there before the Second World War. HMS *Hood* was in the loch in 1935 on manoeuvres and some local people were taken out to see over her, and the stones date from that time. The *Hood* was sunk in the war, with a mere three survivors from a crew of over 1,400 men. Another name is that of HMS *Courageous*, a cruiser in the First World War, adapted then as an aircraft carrier and sunk early in the second war. Other names are thought to be a postwar additions, judging by the condition of the heather around the boulders. These are the *Blake*, a cruiser, the *Swift*, a destroyer, the *Valiant*, a battleship, the *Whirlwind*, a destroyer, the *Normandy*, *Unga*, *Lucretia* and *Johanna*, a Dutch minesweeper. Most recent is the addition of HMS *Sutherland*, a present-day visitor which also established links with the county.

Sutherland has more than one military mystery, and Mr Alan Joyce of Lairg recalls the local tale of Lord Kitchener. Kitchener was killed when, on 5 June 1916, the cruiser HMS *Hampshire* sank off Orkney. There has always been much speculation as to the cause of the sinking. Military historians have never considered the official explanations plausible.

Local memories on this subject recall stories of a man seen loitering on the platform at Euston Station in London, when

Kitchener boarded the overnight train to Thurso to cross to Stromness to join the *Hampshire* in Scapa Flow.

Just before the *Hampshire* was sunk, a man who said that he had cycled from Thurso took the ferry across the Kyle of Tongue to Melness (there was no bridge at that time). The ferryman never took him back and some hours later, children playing at Midfield found clothes and personal effects stuffed down a rabbit hole. No sign of the cycle was ever found. The story is that a German submarine picked up the mysterious cyclist from a sandy beach near the mouth of the Kyle about a mile and a half from Talmine pier. Was he a German spy directing the whole operation?

The island of Eilean Choraidh in Loch Eriboll, Sutherland, is about four miles south-east of Durness on the A838.

A rowing boat which crossed the Atlantic

Of all the boats on the west coast of Scotland, there can be few that have travelled quite so far with only a pair of oars to push them. And there can be few small boats resting now on the west coast – scene of many a tearful exodus from the homeland – which have traversed the Atlantic from west to east.

A boatshed at Ardmore is the resting place of a twenty-four-foot Yorkshire dory, bought for £185. She sports the unlikely name, given the shed and its location at Loch Laxford in north-west Sutherland, of *English Rose III*.

She left Nauset Inlet, Orleans, Massachusetts, USA, on Saturday 4 June 1966 and landed on the Irish coast ninety-two days later. She had been adapted slightly on arrival in the USA on the advice of some elderly local fishermen, whose lives had depended on their own dories in days gone past, and her sides had been raised nine inches and capped with steel.

On board were John Ridgway and Chay Blyth, and although both have now gone on to claim fame with further adventures, the essence of their fame and character lies in the dory, safely tucked away in a 'museum' shed at Ardmore, from where John Ridgway runs his School of Adventure. Chay Blyth, whose experience of sea crossings had been apparently confined to a cross-channel

ferry before the epic transatlantic row, has gone on to circum-
navigate the world in both directions and lead many sailing
challenges.

*Ardmore, Loch Laxford, Sutherland, is between Scourie and Kinlochbervie, five
miles off the main road, the A838, around three miles north of Laxford
Bridge.*

Hidden safely away in a shed beside Loch Laxford in the north-west of
Scotland is the boat in which Chay Blyth and John Ridgway rowed the
Atlantic, a feat which propelled them both into the limelight and gave each
a lifelong interest in sea-faring adventures.

A spectacular gorge and a spectacular bridge

A connection exists between the engineering marvel that is the
massive Forth Railway Bridge, constructed between 1883 and
1890, and the earlier bridge over Corrieshalloch Gorge near
Ullapool.

The Corrieshalloch Gorge suspension footbridge, of much
smaller proportions and of elegant design, with an 'airy hammock
like curve' according to the National Monuments Record of
Scotland, spans a gorge which is about sixty metres deep and
almost a mile long. It was designed by Sir John Fowler, a bridge

builder of renown in the later nineteenth century. He had this bridge built either in 1867, as was usually thought, or perhaps later in 1874. This later date was only found in the 1950s, and names a Mr John Dixon of 1 Lawrence Poutney Hill, London, as the construction engineering builder.

The situation is spectacular, overlooking the Falls of Measach, and both the gorge and bridge are owned by the National Trust for Scotland and are generally open to the public (although the bridge was temporarily closed for repairs in 2005/6). The bridge sways a little over its awesome drop and waterfall below, and as you admire its elegance you may well be standing in the footsteps of Sir John Fowler, who, with Sir Benjamin Baker, designed and built the Forth Bridge, the first major structure made of steel. He bought the estate of Braemore in 1867 and may well have tried out some of his bridge-building ideas in this structure, just ten years before he played his part in the building of the Forth Bridge.

Corrieshalloch Gorge suspension footbridge is twelve miles south of Ullapool on the A835, OS map reference NH203780. The Corrieshalloch Gorge National Nature Reserve and the footbridge are both owned by the National Trust for Scotland, and access details should be available on their website.

9

Places with a touch of magic, retreats and places of refuge

Of wolves and old wifies

The island of Handa is now bereft of permanent human residents, although there is accommodation for temporary visitors who come to carry out any work necessary to maintain Handa as a treasure island for ornithologists.

It is a recognised Site of Special Scientific Interest (SSSI) and is run as a nature reserve by the Scottish Wildlife Trust with well over 170 species of birds, including the 100,000 resident guillemots, along with 216 species of plants and more than 100 mosses. A few hundred years ago, the island was a refuge for man – wolves are said to have been so prevalent in Sutherland that the dead in their coffins were rowed across to the island, as it was deemed the only safe resting place.

Although the island now echoes to the sound of birds, it was home to around sixty-five people in the 1841 census, and records show that twelve families resided there. The islanders existed on a diet of fish, sea birds and their eggs, and potatoes. The birds would be culled by the men, as they were on many of the outer Hebridean islands which have cliffs convenient for nesting. It was a precarious life, here as on St Kilda, but it was the reliance of the residents on potatoes which brought about the final downfall, as the potato blight of 1848 reduced the islanders to starvation, and they left forever.

With their exodus died a distinct culture and way of life, for Handa was ruled by a 'Queen'. She was the island's eldest widow, and she presided each morning as the menfolk met to decide upon the tasks for the day. She was recognised by all as being in charge, and as the last Queen of Handa viewed her final 'parliament', she might or might not have realised that as her traditional reign was ending, the reign of another queen, Victoria, was only just beginning.

Handa, Sutherland, lies two miles north-west from the town of Scourie. The nearest main road is the A894.

A pope, a rector and a duke

Of the many lost and hidden buildings in Scotland, very few can be as romantic and idyllic as the ruins which are Kilneuair Church and graveyard. It features on no tourist map, there is no signpost to indicate where it lies, nor is it visible from the road. It hides many stories, from the long arm of papal influence in medieval times to the stirrings and beginnings of Protestantism and, more recently, the energies of the local Scottish Women's Rural Institutes.

The site of the church overlooks Loch Awe to the north and is but a short few minutes' walk from the lochside road on the south side. The only indication of where to go is the ramshackle remains of a rusty pole, for it is here that the old right of way from Loch Awe to Loch Fyne passes. The road would also have been used as a drove road, a carriage track and as a direct route for the charcoal burners to carry their product over the hills to Furnace for the iron smelting there. Amble up the path to the remains, which stand on a knoll with a clear view to the east and north of Loch Awe, amid a flattish area surrounded by the remains of a wall and edged by huge trees. Inside the ruined church is the font, outside, to the west, are medieval gravestones, one of a knight in armour, although you might have to scrape the vegetation off to see it properly. The official Kilmartin website describes three medieval tapered grave slabs, variously decorated with armed figures, dragon heads, a Latin cross and plant designs. There is also a sixteenth-century tomb chest inside the church with moulded decoration. The entire place is overgrown.

So little was known about the site that the local Scottish Women's Rural Institutes (SWRI) decided to include it in their ambitious project to record the history of the area. They introduced Kilneuair as the great mother church of the parish of Glassary. The SWRI felt that this place was almost certainly an ancient place of worship and founded by St Columba on one of his missionary journeys, and at the very least it was a medieval parish church. Associations with early religious beliefs are also contained in the name, Kilneuair or Cill an Iubhair, which means 'church of the yew tree', yews being symbolic of religious places.

Although the entire area around Kilmartin is steeped in even earlier human history, the first recorded reference to this place is 1394, and the building has been dated as thirteenth century with alterations and additions in the sixteenth century. The SWRI account continues:

> Not very far up the western shore of Loch Awe lies a very ancient burial ground and church site where the Campbell lairds of Inverleiver for many centuries buried their dead. Unlike Kilneuair its name, Kilmoha, is securely enshrined and perpetuated as it bears the name of a saint who was famous in his day, which was the pre-Columbian period.
>
> Therefore it is fair to assume that St Columba founded a church at Kilneuair because the west shores of Loch Awe were already served by Kilmoha Church.

What is known is that two papal mandates are still extant. One was the dismissal of James Scrymgeour in 1423 from his post as rector because he did not understand the local language, Gaelic – very plausible, even if it now seems incredible that such decisions could be taken concerning the goings-on on a remote Scottish lochside from halfway across Europe. In his place, Pope Martin V appointed Nigel, son of Colin Campbell, the contemporary Archdeacon of Argyll, to take over from Scrymgeour who in his year and a half as rector had been so unsuccessful that his parishioners had suffered to 'the danger of their souls'.

A century or so later, another Scrymgeour took up the mantle: Henry, a scholar of the sixteenth century who hailed from Geneva. However, he was not appointed by a papal diktat because much had taken place in the world scene in the intervening period. Henry was swept up in the Protestant movement while travelling in Italy in 1550, converted from Catholicism, and when living in Geneva was one of the signatories of Calvin's testament in 1564. If this story sounds astonishing when viewed amid the bracken and broken stones from the hillock above Loch Awe, the story took another extraordinary twist.

Henry was sixty years old, and of course by now a Protestant and able to marry, which he did to a much younger wife. She died soon after but lived long enough to produce a daughter. The marriage ceremony was performed by Calvin and when the Earl of Dundee visited Geneva in 1964 he was shown the register of marriages in the public library which bore the signature of Calvin himself. The earls of Dundee are descendants of this Henry Scrymgeour.

Kilneuair, Argyll, is a couple of hundred metres from the B840 on the south side of Loch Awe, and approximately one and a half miles from Ford. It is up the old right of way over to Loch Fyne.

Island of Davaar, cave painting

Archibald Mackinnon, the art teacher at Campbeltown Grammar School in the 1880s, was a secretive man with an obsession. He was said to have had a vision of the Crucifixion surrounded by the sins of the world, and decided to paint the scene. Another version states that he undertook a painting of the Crucifixion as an act of piety after a shipwreck.

The canvas he chose was the walls of a cave on the island of Davaar at the entrance to Campbeltown Loch. The people of Kintyre only gradually became aware of this huge mural emerging in the cave. They had no inkling of the identity of the artist, who apparently rowed out to the island or walked out at low tide on the causeway, to work on his masterpiece. When the identity of the painter was discovered, so the story goes, Mackinnon immediately left the area and went south to live in England. The local townspeople spoke admiringly of his work, describing how the eyes of Christ would 'follow you around as you looked'.

Archibald Mackinnon, it was locally rumoured, had disappeared in order to establish himself as a great artist, but he never achieved fame. Many years later, in 1934, he suddenly re-appeared and touched up the painting, before dying the following year.

By the 1950s the painting was in need of further attention and the art master of the time undertook this task, but the paint seeped due to the damp of the cave, and the town raised money in the 1970s to employ a professional artist to restore the work. In the event it was again restored by the then art master at Campbeltown Grammar School, and there it remains to this day. The cave is on the seaward side of the island, and can be approached at low tide by walking on the rocky causeway.

To reach the island of Davaar, take the A83 or the B842 south from Tarbert, Kintyre, in Argyll. From Campbeltown take a secondary road south-east following the coast to Kildalloig, but before reaching this hamlet, the island will be visible on the left. Ask at the Tourist Information Office in Campbeltown for details of tides.

Killochries preaching pillars

The biblical scenes carved on the gateposts at Killochries were commissioned by Boyd Porterfield, a member of one of the oldest families in Renfrewshire, who owned the Duchall estate. They were erected in memory of the Killochries community and the carvings symbolise Zechariah's prophecy of Jesus' triumphant entry into Jerusalem, riding on a donkey.

To have commissioned such evocative pillars in memory of a community suggests a heartfelt cause. It is indeed so. In 1988, Mrs Margaret Ferguson of Bridge of Weir wrote a full account of the church over its turbulent 250-year history.

The background to the story lies in the revolt by various congregations and ministers up and down the country against the issue of patronage, or the insistence of the local laird (and largest holder of the purse strings) that his choice in the appointment of church ministers should be paramount. In 1737, John Fleming was installed as minister at the Old Kirk in Kilmacolm, and although he was unpopular with the congregation, who rejected him, the Earl of Glencairn forced the appointment. The result was that some of the congregation left and applied to the new Secession Church for a minister. Although the Seceders' ostensible complaint was the issue of patronage, others felt that they had broken away from the Established Church because its views were in general becoming too liberal.

The Secessionist group began to meet at Killochries, a farm on the road between Kilmacolm and Lochwinnoch. Described at the time as a 'Five Acre Field' and 'retired, remote, in rural quietude, among hills and streams and melancholy deserts', the quiet fields today nestle between South Newton and Killochries.

The pillars have been moved a short distance from their original site and can be viewed easily from the road about a mile and a half south-west from Kilmacolm at the entrance to Killochries House. The carving on the gateposts is embellished with weaving plants round the stones, and is symbolic rather than realistic.

A doctor's refuge

The gravestone of Dr Elizabeth Blackwell in Kilmun gives a brief account of her life. Why did this lady, who had spent much of her life in America, choose to be buried here? Had she ever lived here? Who exactly was she?

Some of the answers are to be found in the august rooms of the London School of Medicine, where there hangs a portrait of Elizabeth Blackwell, painted after a sketch made by the comtesse de Charnacée in Paris in 1859. Elizabeth Blackwell was the first woman to receive a medical degree, having gained her qualification in America. She was born in 1821, the third daughter of Samuel Blackwell, a Bristol sugar refiner. Hers was a fairly well-to-do upbringing. Her father was a strong believer in equality and supported the freedom of women. His daughters were given the same opportunities as their brothers and a good education. Blackwell abhorred slavery and after the family emigrated to New York in August 1832, the family house became

Elizabeth Blackwell, first woman doctor in America, chose to be buried in Kilmun.

one of those havens sheltering slaves on their way to Canada and freedom.

Although Blackwell's business in New York at first thrived, a calamitous fire wiped out much of his capital and, following a move to Cincinnati in May 1838, the family fortunes waned further, culminating in the sudden death of Elizabeth's adored father on 7 August. With only twenty dollars left to support a family which included nine children, two of the daughters opened a school on 27 August.

But Elizabeth Blackwell was an unhappy teacher, although she could at the time see no other opportunity open to her. One day she was visiting a friend who was dying of a uterine illness. This friend had too long concealed her condition from a doctor, the surgery or treatment for such ailments in those days being riskier than most women would contemplate. Like most women of the era, Elizabeth's friend had been too modest to seek medical help from a male doctor, and too frightened of the appalling treatments then meted out.

'You are fond of study,' she is reported to have said to Elizabeth, 'you have health and leisure, why not study medicine?'

At first Elizabeth dismissed the thought, but after her friend's death, she was haunted by her words. The memory helped her on the long road to finding a college which would admit her as a student. Finally, and after many rejections, the Geneva Medical College in the State of New York accepted her.

Final qualification did not open employment doors, but she went to Paris, working there for a few years until she contracted an eye infection which cost her the sight of one eye and the impairment of the other, and jettisoned her ambition to be a surgeon. Then followed yet more study at St Bartholomew's Hospital in London, and a final return to New York, where she opened her own private practice, later assisted by her sister Emily, who had also qualified in medicine and as a surgeon. Eventually the New York Infirmary of Indigent Women and Children was opened by the sisters.

In the meantime, Elizabeth had given up the idea of marriage, but adopted an orphan, Kitty, who lived with her until her death. The remainder of Elizabeth Blackwell's life was spent in travelling, lecturing and writing, and she eventually settled, after a great deal of restlessness and constant moving, at Rock House in the old section of Hastings, in the south of England. There she lived with Kitty until her death on 31 May 1910.

But she had chosen Kilmun for her burying place when she and Kitty had visited the Cowal Peninsula on holiday, as she had been very attracted to the area. After Elizabeth Blackwell's death, Kitty returned to America and died there in 1936.

Kilmun, Argyll and Bute, is on the A880 about eight miles north of Dunoon. The village overlooks the Holy Loch.

Mull's lost village and caves with secrets: an illicit whisky still and hidden hen houses

There are many abandoned villages deep in the hill country of the Islands and Highlands of Scotland, all with a tale to tell. Some were abandoned abruptly in a matter of weeks during the Clearances in the early nineteenth century. People whose roots went back for generations were wrenched out of their homes by brute force, or forceful persuasion, depending on the landlord or his appointee, frequently leaving houses in a relatively good condition. Other villages were gradually abandoned as the people migrated to the towns or voluntarily moved to other parts of the mainland or abroad. No one seems to be sure why the village of Crackaig was deserted, but probably its location reveals all.

The setting is idyllic today, with its roofless houses huddled in a neighbourly fashion looking south to wide romantic views across to Staffa and the Hebrides. It is one of my favourite abandoned villages.

The only remaining tree sits inside an enclosure which may have been the communal garden. Round many of the houses are still to be seen the flat pavement stones. The buildings are in remarkably good condition, considering they were possibly abandoned more than 150 years ago. A total lack of slates points to the roofs being made of traditional turf or heather.

Crackaig was not just a village which relied on fishing, egg collecting and the meagre produce of the soil. To find another secret of its economy, you must strike north from the village, following the edge of the cliff until you see a sort of a track, only 200 metres from the village, leading down eventually to the beach. This is a steep walk, but a safe one. Do not take the first available descent on leaving the village as it is dangerous.

Keep north on the beach until you come to a deep cave. Inside this cave was a very effective still for distilling whisky. P. A. Macnab, a Mull man who has written extensively about the island, reports that he used to be able to find the remains of whisky bottles there, but to discover one today would be a lucky find indeed. The location of the still had one purpose: to evade the searching and spying eyes of the ever-watchful Excise cutters which plied up and down the coast.

The black pot and the 'worm' were probably made by the local blacksmith. A turf wall was built along the front to hide the glow of the furnace from any passing curious boat; any smoke blended with the hills behind. A tiny stream was diverted across the front of the cave at the right distance to cool the 'worm'.

The quality of the whisky must have been good, for the local fishermen and operators used to sail all the way to Ireland where there was a good market for their product.

They must have been skilful sailors, and their reliance on the sea is also commemorated. To the right of one of the doors into a ruined house has been carved an outline of a sailing boat, with the date of 1861 and name James (with the S the wrong way round) McCay. Reudle School, a tall, severe, dark stone house, operated as a school only between around 1860 and 1877, being superseded by the 'new' school at Kilninian, down the coast, after which it gradually fell into ruin. The graffiti on the walls confirmed these dates, with drawings of ships and initials scratched onto the plaster.

Another series of caves, also converted with a purpose, can still be seen on the shore between Laggan and Rudha Liath. For many years the roughly built stone walls blocking the entrances were a puzzle to local historians, and the secret might well have been lost had they not heard the tale from a lady whose family had lived and worked in the area for over 100 years. In the 1800s the ownership of the estate had passed into a family who forbade the women, who traditionally kept hens in rural areas, to continue with the practice. Much depended on poultry in remote areas and all small agricultural holdings kept them. Eggs were stored for months over the winter in water with isinglass; surplus eggs could be sold; feathers were used in pillows if duck could not be found; and finally, any hen past its useful laying life became a meal for celebration. Meat was not a daily item on the dinner table for any but the wealthy. So not surprisingly, the hens were deemed too important to lose, and no doubt the wily women would have guessed that by concealing the hens in caves, not only would they be out of the usual walking route of the occupants of the big house, but the noise of the sea would muffle any give-away cackling.

Crackaig, on the island of Mull, can be found on the B8073 about five miles south of Calgary Bay. The abandoned village of Crackaig is clearly marked on the OS map reference NM351462. The simplest method of finding this village is to park by the schoolhouse at Reudle, again well marked, where you will see a footpath which leads to the schoolhouse and then beyond. Follow this until you see the first village on the right, preceded by what looks like the remains of a man-made dam, perhaps for the conservation of fresh water, and then proceed to a V or dip in the land where the small burn goes through the gap. To the right is the village of Crackaig.

The Falls of Clyde and the mirrored pavilion

The gorge which contains the Falls of Clyde was much visited in the nineteenth century, and it has been a tourist attraction for well over 200 years. Lavish praise was heaped on the beauty of the falls as early as the seventeenth century, and this led to the erection by Sir James Carmichael of Bonnington in 1708 of a viewing

A 200-year-old tourist attraction, this pavilion at the Falls of Clyde was originally mirrored to give added drama to the scene of rushing water below.

pavilion. To dramatise the rush and power of the falls, the rear wall of the pavilion was hung with a mirror. This structure must have been a considerable attraction in 1708. Mirrors were a prized and expensive commodity in those days and to use them in such a pleasure house was very unusual.

The First Statistical Account (1791–9) states:

> from its uppermost room, it affords a very striking prospect of the Fall, for all at once, on turning your eyes towards a mirror on the opposite side of the room from the fall, you see the whole tremendous cataract pouring as it were upon your head.

There was, however, some criticism of the pavilion and the placing of the mirror, and a more jaundiced account is less enthusiastic. Leighton wrote:

> the illusion is not so perfect as it might obviously be. The mirror is neither of sufficient size or of a proper shape or sufficiently concealed in the wall. Were a little expense laid out in this pavilion ...

By 1835 things had seemingly improved: 'Mirrors are suspended throughout the room by looking into which the tremendous cataract seems ready to burst forth,' and the pavilion was 'well provided with chairs and there is a register here in which tourists enter their names and addresses'.

Look up at the ruined pavilion now and you see one of the early attempts to harness the tourist trade. The view was exaggerated, and the intention, as in today's audio-visual presentations, was to offer a mixture of grandeur and spine-tingling amazement, to thrill the punters. Now roofless, this early attempt to exploit one of Scotland's natural wonders is but a ruined fragment of its former glory.

The Scottish Wildlife Trust now manages the Falls of Clyde Reserve and they are based in the former Dyeworks in New Lanark. To find New Lanark, which is south-west of Lanark, take the M74 south from Glasgow to Junction 9. Take the A744 which joins up with the A72 to Lanark. The distance from leaving the M74 is about six miles.

Hamilton's echoing mausoleum

The Hamilton Mausoleum sits aloof from the roar of the nearby M74, easily visible from the passing vehicles. It is often visited, but for a reason which its larger-than-life builder never anticipated, since he died before the building's completion. The reason is that it has probably the longest echo of any building in the country.

No other mausoleum in Scotland seems to have been built on the massive scale of this one. Constructed for Alexander, tenth Duke of Hamilton (1767–1852), it was not complete at the time of his death. The building commenced in 1842 and took fifteen years to complete, at a cost of £30,000.

The tenth duke was aptly nicknamed 'Il Magnifico'. He built Hamilton Palace, now demolished, on a site just south of the

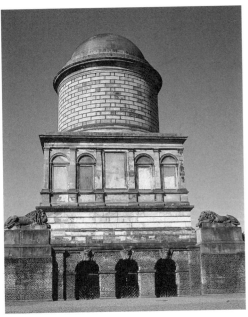

Built by the then Duke of Hamilton in the 1840s, and taking fifteen years to complete, the Mausoleum of the duke himself is clearly visible from the nearby M74 south of Glasgow. Guarded by huge stone lions, and designed by architect David Bryce to house the man who thought he was the rightful heir to the throne of Scotland, it claims to have the longest echo of any building in the British Isles.

mausoleum. It was not far from the truth to describe the palace as one of the most magnificent piles in the kingdom. Other sources went so far as to say that it was one of the most outstanding palaces in the world, which is nearer to what the duke fervently wished. There was an impulsive and generous streak in his nature. For example, when the ninth duke's will stipulated that all his personal possessions should go to his younger daughter, this meant that his younger son was excluded from the inheritance; the new duke immediately gave his younger brother £20,000.

The tenth duke regarded himself as the rightful heir to the throne of Scotland, and although he made no moves towards effecting a claim, he set about housing himself in an edifice worthy of his status. In addition to being Duke of Hamilton he also held three marquisates, three earldoms and eight baronies.

However, his vast palace had a short life. In 1882 the contents were sold and the house itself was demolished in 1920, as a result, it was always said, of subsidence from coal mining – a supreme irony since revenue from coal was one of the foundations upon which the Hamilton fortune had been built. This explanation was later disputed, and the reasons for the demolition were probably also financial.

But to return to the mausoleum. The architect was David Bryce and he designed a burial place fit for, if not a king, then amply fit for a duke who thought he should be a king. The building stands more than thirty-six metres high, and the walls and their construction are remarkable. Each huge stone is dovetailed into its neighbour virtually without mortar; it is said that less than a ton of lime was used in the whole building. The lower part of the building, the vaulted basement, holds the entrance to the crypt. The top of the stairs is guarded by two colossal lions, one awake, one asleep, sculpted by Alexander Handyside Ritchie of Edinburgh.

The duke had removed some of his ancestors from the old churchyard of the fifteenth-century collegiate church at Hamilton in order to make room for improvements on his land, but long after his death and just after the demolition of the palace they were re-buried in Bent Cemetery, Hamilton (also the resting place of Sir Harry Lauder).

As the duke had built to a grand scale for his mortal life, so too he planned the details of his life after death. In 1836 he bought in Paris, on behalf of the British Museum, a sarcophagus which should have contained the remains of an ancient Egyptian queen. However, when it arrived at the British Museum it was found to contain a lady without royal descent, called Iret-irw. The duke immediately offered to reimburse the museum and keep the sarcophagus himself. They accepted, and the sum of £632 8s. 6d. changed hands. By all accounts, the duke spent some time trying it out for size. Not surprisingly, it was too small for 'Il Magnifico', and he instructed stonemasons to chisel enough out to ensure that he would fit into it. His last journey was to purchase the spices for his embalmment. However, despite all these preparations, his final resting place is not inside the mausoleum which he planned for so many years, but in the family plot at Bent Cemetery.

When the outer wooden doors of the mausoleum, protecting the bronze inner doors (facsimiles of the Ghiberti doors at the Baptistery of Florence), clang shut, the reverberating echoes can be clearly heard. It is a great irony that this place of worship cannot be used for purposes of worship on account of its acoustics. Whispers in one of the alcoves of the octagonal chapel can be distinctly heard in the opposite corner. One person singing becomes the sound of a choir.

The chapel contains eight niches, which were either to be filled with statues of the twelve apostles or twelve successive dukes of Hamilton. It matters little today, as after the tenth duke died, the chapel was left unfinished.

The Hamilton Mausoleum near Glasgow can be reached by taking the M74 south from Glasgow (about ten miles from the centre of Glasgow) and leaving at Junction 6. The mausoleum is on the west side of the M74, about a couple of miles from the motorway by road.

Leadhills, tombstone of John Taylor

The tombstone of John Taylor, a surveyor in the lead mines of the area, states that his age when he died was 137. He had no birth certificate, and apparently he could have been just 134, but who would want to quibble? Certainly not the local authority who are presumably responsible for erecting the sign at the entrance to the graveyard indicating his gravestone, other occupiers of the graveyard being overlooked as they all seem to have shuffled off their mortal coil at well under the century.

Local legend has it that Taylor's family took him to the top of the nearest and highest hill, the one now topped by a radar station, when he was 100 years old, so that God could catch sight of him and be reminded to call him into His fold. The legend offers no other explanation for carting such an aged man to the top of any hill on his birthday. However, God must have been looking the other way as John Taylor had to wait another 34 or 37 years to be called to his maker.

Leadhills is about fifteen miles north-west of Moffat. On the A74, take the exit at A702 (Elvanfoot) and then immediately branch onto the B7040 for about six miles.

Nelson's monument

Long after Christianity had become the established religion, stone circles still commanded a somewhat backhand respect. On the one hand they symbolised a lost, ancient and suspiciously pagan rite. On the other hand, it was considered downright foolish to remove too many of them, perhaps tempting fate to drop bad luck upon the remover.

Many single standing stones, visible all over the country, were once one of a circle. Gradually over the centuries, as farming methods improved, machinery arrived which was more easily able to shift these massive slabs of stone, but it was the rare farmer who dared to remove them all. One single stone was often left, alone and respected. In the last fifty years, I cannot recall the disappearance of a single lonesome standing stone. Old habits die hard. Standing proud in a field, and no doubt cursed by a farmer ploughing or harrowing as he manoeuvres his ever larger machinery round about it, it still remains. Most are now numbered, protected and in any case sunk deep into the ground, but even before this documenting began, they were generally left in peace.

For a stone to be shifted took an event of overriding and huge importance. One particular stone, at Taynuilt, was moved, not because it was in the way of anyone nor because it interfered with the Christian settlements close by, but because of Horatio Nelson. And it was moved a full mile, long before the arrival of the internal combustion engine could offer assistance.

North of the parish church at Taynuilt, on the aptly named Cnoc Aingeal or Hill of the Fires, stands this stone, with an inscription commemorating the Battle of Trafalgar.

To the memory of Lord Nelson
this stone was erected by
Lorn Furnace workmen, 1805.

Even in the 1820s, the removal provoked a frosty response. The entry comments:

on the arrival of the intelligence of the victory obtained by Lord Nelson over the French Fleet at Aboukir, the workmen at the Lorn furnace, not in the best possible taste, removed this obelisk to the neighbouring hill, where it yet remains having been the first monument probably raised in commemoration of that victory.

Later, the journal of the Society of Antiquities of Scotland (vol. 61; sixth series, vol. 1) noted that the stone cabar sits on the long low ridge bearing the name of Barran nan Cabar, the field also being known as the Moine a Charrach ('moss of the pillar'):

[the] Cabar or Carragh was a large prone monolith of grey granite, 16 feet by 3 feet broad by 1 foot thick. It may originally have been a solitary standing stone or part of a circle. . . . The iron workers at the furnace had mounted the four ton block on wooden rollers, and dragged it a mile eastward.

The iron workers had good cause to celebrate. It was their foundry which had helped supply the cannonballs and shot which were used by the army and navy in the war.

Taynuilt is on the A85 around eight miles east from Connel. The stone is now hidden from view of the main road by the houses and shops in Taynuilt.

Innellan and the hymn with hidden meaning

Scotland has produced some heroic and charismatic churchmen, many of whom have worked on behalf of, or given their lives to helping, the oppressed, poor and deserving, but behind the words of the hymn 'O love that will not let me go' is a deeper, more personal meaning, which came out of great private pain, and which has little to do with religious niceties.

Sung on Jerusalem's Hill of Calvary in the Sunday School Convention of 1904 by representatives of twenty-six different nations, it was a tribute to its composer, Dr George Matheson, who penned the words on the evening of 6 June 1882 in the Manse at Innellan, the day before his sister's wedding.

George Matheson was one of the great preachers and pastors in the tradition of the Presbyterian Church. Born in March 1842, the son of a well-to-do Glasgow merchant, he was highly gifted, a poet, and fortunate enough to be able to live in an area which he had fallen in love with during his childhood holidays. He lived there for eighteen years. His path had been set fair. He graduated with honours from Glasgow University in 1862, followed by the degree of Doctor of Divinity from Edinburgh twelve years later. He came as the local minister to Innellan in 1868. Such was his popularity that when he was expected home to the newly constructed manse at Innellan from trips to Glasgow, young lads would be sent down to watch the arrivals off the steamers, and when he arrived send round word, and this guaranteed his church would be packed the following Sunday.

Matheson was no hellfire preacher. His sermons rarely lasted more than twenty minutes, and his outlook was liberal and very enlightened for the age. Not for him the rigid beliefs of some contemporaries. He argued that acceptance of the theory of evolution tended to strengthen belief in Christianity, as 'the supernatural creation is in the heart of man, and must have existed long before the historical Christ', brave and bold words so soon after Darwin's theory of evolution had stirred up storms of controversy.

Matheson had a sense of humour; private prayer caused him no anxieties, as he knew he was talking to God; on the other hand, he declared, 'when I preach the devil might be among the congregation!' He visited his parishioners and he worked to raise money for the church spire. His hobby was poetry and he would only be able to compose when standing in some of the local favourite beauty spots. All in all he was a model minister. As he stood each Sunday in church to read from the Bible, and walked over to the rostrum, his thoughts were to reassure his congregation, because George Matheson was blind, and he would always ask that the Bible was open at the correct verse, as it put his congregation at their ease. He would have memorised the passage previously, just as he had memorised hymns and psalms.

The fact of his blindness, poor sight worsening during his teenage years until he suffered total sight loss at eighteen, made his many achievements astonishing. But it was the confirmation that his sight would never get better which led to him writing his favourite hymn, 'O Love that will not let me go'.

On the eve of his sister's wedding, when he was also looking forward to his own marriage, he had offered his fiancée her freedom from their engagement, as he had just received the confirmation of his irreversible sight loss. When she accepted he was heartbroken, and penned the hymn as his memorial to his love for her. So the hymn which was one of the church's most popular for many decades was in fact an ode to his lost love. Little did his congregation realise that their minister George Matheson and Rabbie Burns had much in common (from *Innellan*, by the Revd John C. Hill, 1943).

Innellan, Argyll, is on the A815 four miles south of Dunoon.

Healing waters at Loch Maree

One of the traditional skills of St Maelrubha, the patron saint of Morisons of Ness, was his ability as the special healer of lunacy. A belief in the healing virtues of the well in Inch Maree (Mourie or

Maelrubha) probably still lingers in the west of Ross-shire (W. C. Mackenzie, in *The History of the Outer Hebrides*, 1903).

In former times it was a common practice to bring those supposed to be lunatics to Loch Maree to be cured. Similarly, patients were taken from many parts of the north-west of Scotland to the church at Ness, with the same object in mind. The patient walked seven times round the building, was sprinkled with water from St Ronan's Well, which was close at hand, and was then bound and left for the night on the site of the altar. In the morning the 'patients' would be unbound and safely retrieved from the site, hopefully cured by their exposure to the healing waters and close encounter with the well.

Loch Maree, Wester Ross, is about six miles south-west of Gairloch on the A832.

Island of Inch Kenneth, by Mull

The island of Inch Kenneth was for hundreds of years sought out by various owners for its magical atmosphere and as a retreat from the world – a contrast to the steep cliffs and huge rocks on the road just before the turning down to the pier where the 'Tragedy Rock' commemorates a landslide of rock which landed on top of a cottar house, rumoured to have killed a shepherd and his new wife on their wedding night. The rock is still surrounded by the remains of the dry-stone walls.

Standing down on this pier and looking over to the lush greenness of the island of Inch Kenneth is the tall eighteenth-century house, and a little to the side is a small chapel. This chapel, like so many on the Hebridean islands, has stood for many centuries. Indeed Martin Martin, a great traveller and one of the first diarists and travel writers, penned an account of it: 'The chapel built around 13th century, and was indeed fruitful in cattle and corn ... Little chapel of this Isle many of the inhabitants of all ranks are buried' (Martin Martin, 1703).

Named, possibly, after one of St Columba's followers, Cainneach, the island had become a useful granary, being very fertile. The lease of the island had been held by one of the

Macleans before Johnson and Boswell visited in 1773. This particular Maclean, Sir Allan, had been a soldier from the age of seventeen, first in the Netherlands and then in America. He was given a captain's commission and a regiment composed largely of Jacobite clansmen. His wife died in 1760, after which he returned home to provide for his daughters, for whom he leased the island of Inch Kenneth, where he lived until his death in 1783.

When Johnson and Boswell stepped ashore (later describing it as 'verdant and grassy, but no trees') they were met by Sir Allan, who described how the family lived in a small cottage, but with all the trappings of a civilised life. The guests were duly impressed, recording the house possessing 'unexpected neatness and convenience'.

In the late 1930s and '40s, the house became the wartime retreat of Lady Redesdale, mother of the Mitford sisters. Her support of Hitler estranged her from her husband, and she lived there with Unity, a daughter who had shot herself with a pistol given to her by Hitler and who was as a result severely brain damaged. Lady Redesdale had crisp new £1 and £5 notes posted to her from her bank at Harrods, which she then used to buy goods on Mull.

Today the island is still in private hands.

Inch Kenneth lies within the western channel of Loch na Keal on the west coast of the Isle of Mull. To view the island, and indeed the Tragedy Rock, take the B8035 about nineteen miles from Salen.

Cille Choirille Church, Glen Roy

The fairytale church of Cille Choirille, standing in a breathtaking position up a very steep slope overlooking Glen Roy, has seen much history pass by. It is surrounded by a graveyard with many shapes and varieties of stones dug into the sharply undulating land. It is a place for contemplation, and sited on the east-facing gable-end wall is an idiosyncratically, and fairly recently, carved wooden seat honouring Scottish mountaineer and broadcaster Tom Weir and his wife.

They too must have loved the peace and solitude of this place, with its lengthy views down onto Loch Laggan, but dig not too deep, for others of a more blood-thirsty nature lie here.

The chapel was built around the fifteenth century by a Cameron chief, Ailean nam Creach, as a penance for acts of violence. Not far from the same eastern gable-end against which the Weirs' commemorative bench is placed is an imposing burial stone which commemorates Iain Lom (John MacDonald), Gaelic poet (*c.*1625–post 1707; his exact dates are unknown). He became the first and only Gaelic Poet Laureate, to Charles I. Needless to say, by the time of the Union of the Crowns in 1707, he was openly denouncing such a sell-out on the part of the Scots. He survived such open criticisms, though, and died in relatively old age, roughly in his seventies, and is buried in the graveyard of Cille Choirille.

Much more recently, the church became a focal point for parish services of a very different type, being frequently seen in the popular BBC TV series *Monarch of the Glen*. It is particularly remembered for the scene in which the central character, Archie, is temporarily jilted. Visitors often include some from far afield who have come to feel part of the area through watching the series, which ended in 2005.

Cille Choirille Church is about six miles east along the A86 from Spean Bridge. The church is situated up a small signposted road, steeply inclining, with plenty of parking adjacent to the graveyard and church.

Ardclach Tower, Moray

Only a few miles from the desolate moorland of Dava Moor and the menacing castle of the Wolf of Badenoch at Lochindorb, this tower sits above a church in a flat oasis of tranquillity. The road itself stops there, alongside this sadly unused church, and close by is a lazy bend of the River Findhorn. The river curves round in a classic horseshoe shape, with a great bronze peaty pool, perfect for resting salmon.

Descending this steep road, you pass close by this curious, miniature tower house. Constructed in 1655, two centuries after the death of the Wolf of Badenoch, life appeared a little more civilised, though the builder of Ardclach, Alexander Brodie of Letham, had lost much of his land, forfeited by the Marquis of Montrose. So his new house was a mere but and ben with the addition of height. Even with such a lack of usable living space, he could not resist, rather prudently, creating a basement prison in the event of an opportunity to pay back his accusers. Two centuries on again, in 1832, the bell tower was added, so that the faithful could hear more clearly a summons from atop a hill, rather than the old church in the hollow.

This fast-flowing river must have seen many escapades close to this point. No doubt the Wolf of Badenoch must have crossed it many times, but much earlier a Celtic princess is supposed to have fallen in and drowned trying to elope with her lover, a Danish prince. In the private grounds of Glenferness House to the north is the carved Princess Stone, close to a cairn marking her grave.

Another curious fact is revealed by the memorial to the Revd John Mitchell, born in 1792, the son of the parish minister, who became the first missionary to India to create a leper mission, maintained to this day by the Church of Scotland. A replica of his Indian gravestone sits beside the old bell tower driveway.

To find Lochindorb Castle, which is situated in the midst of the loch of the same name, leave Carrbridge on the A938 going east until a junction with the B9007. Take this road about six miles until another small, unmarked turning takes you across this magnificent moorland a couple of miles. To find Ardclach Bell Tower, retrace your steps back to the B9007, turn right and north to the crossroads with the A939, turn left onto this road, and the sign for the Bell Tower is a mile further on the left.

Seminary and heather priests at Samalaman

The track to the tiny hamlet of Smirisary at Glenuig, Lochailort, takes you past a large white house, which has the appearance, surrounded as it is by agricultural buildings, of a traditional early-eighteenth-century farmhouse.

Not so. Samalaman House was the site of a Roman Catholic seminary, operating between 1783 and 1803. From here roving 'heather priests', so called because they were itinerant and slept where they could, ministered to an isolated rural flock, keeping a low profile. (This is also Bonnie Prince Charlie country, and Roman Catholicism was a dangerous persuasion in the aftermath of the 1745 Jacobite Rebellion.)

Straddling the stream just after the house is a miniature stone house, the skeletal roof of which still reveals rough poles as the basic structure for a covering of heather or turf. Local chat reckons this was the privy for Samalaman House. It would have been a long walk from the house in the middle of a winter's night! Much more likely is that it is an eel house, and most probably the only surviving one of its type on the west coast of Scotland.

Heather priests were few and their wanderings on foot to the most remote hamlets meant that a visit from a priest was a rare and special occurrence for people whose beliefs had left them bereft of a permanent priestly presence.

It is possible to get an inkling of what this type of isolation was really like by walking just a mile or two further on from the house. Following the track onwards, you eventually reach a village lost in time, the scattered hamlets of Smirisary. Perched higgledy-piggledy in the curve of the various small glens leading down to the shore are tiny houses, mostly now with corrugated iron roofs on their rounded walls, held down with ropes weighted with stones. Reached only by footpath or boat, this must be truly one of the most atmospheric rural retreats in Britain.

Owing to the small scale of these old black houses, Smirisary is a made-to-measure child-sized village to explore, with idyllic sandy beaches over the rise. On this very gentle walk there is even a miniature wooden bus shelter. The wind has only allowed the trees to be stunted, the hillocks and path are small scale. The village itself, which unfolds as you walk down, reveals more and more cottages. In days gone by parents could stand on the top rise and keep every playing child within sight.

Smirisary, Inverness-shire, is about twelve miles south-west of the junction between the A830 Mallaig to Fort William road and the A861. At Glenuig on this road, take the turning to the west along a side road, passing the white Samalaman House, until this road peters out, then park and walk along the clearly signed footpaths.

Carsaig on the island of Mull

This is a very feminine area in many ways. It is home both to the red telephone box at Pennyghael which featured in an iconic postwar film *I know where I'm going* with Wendy Hillier, and to the Nuns' Cave, just round the corner at Carsaig, named after the nuns who sheltered here, having been evicted from Iona Abbey after the Reformation. The telephone box still exists, and in summer is surrounded by the ruby red flowers of free-growing wild fuchsias.

Pennyghael is on the A849 on the south side of the island of Mull. The turning down to Carsaig is off the A849, at a junction which is about sixteen miles east of Fionnphort and the Iona crossing. The road is steep and winding.

Poltalloch, the Sleeping Beauty house

Way in the distance over rich meadow fields and sitting as though in a dream-like theatrical set for *Sleeping Beauty*, is the fairytale ivy-clad, mellow ruin of Poltalloch House. It is highly unlikely that any inhabitant of this ruin will be awakened by a youthful prince passing by, but the story of this colossal house did attract a youthful Michael Davis.

For about twenty years Michael has been researching a book on Poltalloch Estate. Today, the rump of this once enormous West Highland estate centres around the evocative and monumental ruin of Poltalloch House, near Kilmartin in mid-Argyll. He describes Poltalloch House as one of those almost unbelievably glamorous 'lifestyle architecture' palaces that a very few super-rich Victorians were able to build, and a few others received invitations to visit; its shelf-life was characteristically short. Completed in the mid-1850s after less than a decade of intense planning and building activity, it saw out only one hundred years before it was unroofed in the late 1950s.

The story of the mansion and its estate may not be well known to the general public, but those who search for and find this vast and stately ruin, or who simply come across it as they explore, discover the first part of a jigsaw that can help to unlock secrets

Poltalloch House, now in ruins. Few family histories are as dramatic as that of the Malcolms of Poltalloch, whose business interests spread as far as Jamaica, and whose family members included the daughter of Lillie Langtry, actress and mistress of Edward, Prince of Wales (the future King Edward VII).

that explain the role of its lairds, the Malcolms of Poltalloch, not only in forming the landscape, but also in engineering the society that inhabited it.

'This was an estate that at its height stretched for almost forty miles in a continuous line,' explains Michael.

The wealth of the Malcolms, originally small-scale landowners and petty chieftains under Campbell suzerainty, was won between the mid-eighteenth and the mid-nineteenth centuries on global market places, from Jamaica to Australia, by means of commodities as diverse as sugar, rum, molasses, cattle, ships and shipping, insurance, very possibly slaves, and – of course – money itself, which was carefully invested or loaned out to make more.

What makes the story of Poltalloch even more interesting is the way it illuminates and helps explain a number of issues which affect not just the rather magical landscapes of mid-Argyll, but of the Highlands as a whole, from estate 'improvement' through the emotive subject of 'Clearances' to the high point – and decline – of Country House life and society.

Unsurprisingly, when he gives lectures, Michael is occasionally asked how he came to tackle this rich and largely unexplored vein of material. His customary answer reveals at root not some weighty academic impulse, but an atmospheric encounter with the past. He explains:

> As a teenager I sailed a lot with Ardrishaig Sailing Club on Loch Fyne. One day, on a long distance race, the rudder of my sailing dinghy broke, and unseen by the rest of the fleet or by the rescue boat, I slowly drifted onto the Cowal shore.

He found an estate track which led eventually to a large empty baronial house. It is, in some ways, another story (for this was not Poltalloch), but it was not just the architecture of that particular house, but also the setting, and the magic of a house clearly abandoned in now overgrown but once intricate gardens, that sparked off an enthusiasm with a sudden intensity. 'It took years for me to get around to tended gardens and maintained buildings! They seemed much too tame and dull at first,' he admits.

It didn't take long before someone told Michael about Poltalloch. It was off the beaten track, but if you got in range of it, it was difficult to miss, or forget. Today, you can get the best view from a minor public road just to the south, which saves any need for an expedition across private land.

> I remember my first visit to find it. I persuaded my father to drive me, but once within the former park he temporarily lost his bearings – he had last been there when it still had a roof – and we stopped to ask a wee boy on a trike for directions to 'the ruin'. He looked mystified at first. Eventually the penny dropped – 'Oh, you mean the Big House' – and he pointed across a field toward where, squinting against the slanting sunlight of a late summer evening, we could make out the silhouette of the vast, creeper-draped, roofless shell of Poltalloch.

Intrigued, Michael began to research the long and remarkable history of the Malcolms – the family whose descendants still own this house – and the social history of their estate. Between writing other studies, he has returned to, but never quite finished, his research. He found that the story of the Malcolms has taken many turns, and a fortuitous marriage in the eighteenth century certainly helped, when the ninth laird, Alexander Malcolm, married a wife who eventually brought Jamaican property to the family. This investment, which sent various members of the family scurrying over to the island to attend to their sugar plantations, and the attendant problems of slavery, was quite some time in developing, and did not produce a generous return for many years. Jamaican slave uprisings and the American War of Independence hampered advancement. Tireless reinvestors of capital, the family slowly built up their prestige, occupying a series of town houses in London and country houses in the south of England. Yet visiting Scotland, despite the lack of comfort both on the journey and in a suitable house in Argyll, was at least a yearly ritual. There, the family involved themselves in farming, tree planting, the improvement of land, and helped to fund the Crinan Canal. Draining a vast area of bogland near the mouth of the Add was by any standards a hugely expensive project, but reaped rewards in the short term. Between 1796 and 1799 the value of the crop had increased fivefold. And, of course, they bought land, and more and more land.

The family continued to advance socially. In London, their house at 7 Great Stanhope Street possessed a garden which backed onto Park Lane. But Scotland was still their homeland, and by the mid-1840s, the laird of the day, Neill Malcolm, began to plan not just an ambitious house, but one which would absorb a fortune. For this enterprise, William Burn, one of the foremost architects of the day, was employed to build a very grand house indeed, so large and imposing that Neill Malcolm himself felt it at first to be 'uncomfortably large'. An adjacent Episcopal chapel was designed by Thomas Cundy, who had already created the ultra-fashionable church of St Paul's, Knightsbridge.

When this large mansion, minutely designed by Burn to accommodate every wish and comfort of the many guests, was completed, its delights ranged from a huge glassed conservatory containing palms and dracenas to dozens of glass cases containing every species of bird native to Britain. The family and their fortunate guests settled down to enjoy life in what was described as a sportsman's paradise. The intriguing, complex and well-thought-out design of the house provided a social hub for the family in what was known as the Corridor, the wide and generous central hall of the house.

Mary Malcolm, a daughter of the house, who went on to become one of the first television presenters in the 1950s, recalled in her book *Me*, an idyllic childhood spent visiting Poltalloch in the 1930s, although even she, who loved it 'more deeply than any place I know' was unable to call it a beautiful building: the denigration of anything Victorian was then in full flow. But it is clear that even in the 1930s the house functioned successfully, with basement service areas and public rooms for various times of the day which followed the sun. Within the walls, and amid the miles of corridors and rooms designed for every occasion, from dining to shooting, accommodating guests and their staff, the children would gather, to the chagrin of their mother, in the Corridor, where large logs would burn in the outsize fireplace, the room dimly lit by a huge stained-glass window. As a child arriving from London for holidays, Mary would retrieve her very own West Highland terrier, Sodger, from Mrs Wills, the keeper's wife, and immerse herself in the grounds of the great house. Sodger was one of the special Poltalloch Westies bred by her grandfather, and still a distinct breed today. She recalled that before the Tenants Ball at Christmas, the children were permitted to slide down the great staircase banister in order to polish it, and she once calculated that food must have travelled a quarter of a mile from the kitchens to the dining room.

Sheena Carmichael, who now lives not far distant, by Ford on the banks of Loch Awe, used to play with Mary, her father being the butler until his death in 1928. As butler to Sir Ian Malcolm, he would have met the many famous people of the time who came to visit, from leading politicians to the King of Iraq.

Glamour had also knocked at the door, since Lillie Langtry was Mary Malcolm's grandmother, though it is not known if the famous beauty managed to get over the threshold! Lillie Langtry, nicknamed 'the Jersey Lily' in honour of her birthplace on the island of Jersey, became both famous and infamous, as an actress and as the mistress of the Prince of Wales. It was she who indirectly added a dash of salacious interest to the long story of the Malcolms, for Lillie's daughter, Jeanne Marie, whom Sir Ian had married in 1902, was reputed to have as her father neither the Prince of Wales, nor indeed Lillie's husband Edward, but Prince Louis of Battenburg, who was to marry into the royal family by wedding a daughter of Queen Victoria.

Scotland hides many stories, but few are as wide-ranging and grand as that of the Malcolms of Poltalloch. Despite their grandeur and connections, death duties and a lack of success in making money meant that by the 1950s the estate was shrinking, and the day of reckoning for the great house could not be postponed. Having further to fall than most, the ultimate unroofing and stripping of the mansion seemed symbolic of the end not just of the Malcolms' luxurious palace, but of a way of life. Yet the Malcolms survived this seeming cataclysm with remarkable verve, retrenching to smaller holdings centred on nearby Duntrune Castle, where they are still.

The ruin of Poltalloch House, however, survives as not just a memorial to a lost fortune, but in its own right, as one of the most impressive visions of a forgotten and hidden Scotland.

Poltalloch is south-west of Kilmartin, Argyll. Poltalloch House stands on private land, but can be viewed easily from a distance from the B8025. Take the A816 south from Oban for about twenty-nine miles, passing through Kilmartin, and take the B8025 west. After a mile or so, you can see the bulk of Poltalloch in the distance across fields. The church stands slightly to the east of the main house.

Bibliography

Most of the material in the book is based on independent research and appeared originally in articles published in the *Scots Magazine* over a period of twelve years. The following is a list of specific works cited in the text:

Anderson, W., *The Howes o' Buchan,* (Peterhead, 1865)

Christie, E., *The Empty Shore: The Story of Cowie, Kincardineshire,* (Dundee, 1974)

Gregor, W., *Notes on the Folk-lore of the North-east of Scotland* (Edinburgh, 1881)

Gunn, C. B., *Leaves from the Life of a Country Doctor* (Edinburgh, 2002)

Hamilton, F., *Kipper House Tales* (Ardrishaig, 1986)

Hill, J. C., *Innellan* (Innellan, 1943)

Lennon, P., *The Tale of the Mouse: The Life and Work of Robert Thompson the Mouseman of Kilburn* (Ilkley, 2001)

Macdonald, J., *Sketches of May* (Bowmore, 1996)

Mackenzie, W. C., *The History of the Outer Hebrides* (Paisley, 1903)

MacLeod, D., *Oasis of the North: A Highland Garden* (London, 1963)

Malcolm, H. M., *Me* (London, 1956)

Maxwell, G., *Ring of Bright Water* (London, 1960)

Mitchell, A., *The Past and the Present* (Edinburgh, 1832)

Mitchell, Sir A., *Past in the Present: What is Civilisation?* (Edinburgh, 1862)

Ochterlony, J. *Account of the Shire of Forfar, circa 1682* (Forfar, 1969)

Rickman, J., *Laird of the Light Houses* (published by author, 1994)

Shearer, J., *Antiquities of Strathearn* (Crieff, 1883)

Somerville, A. R., *The Ancient Sundials of Scotland* (London, 1994)

Stansfield, J., *The Story of Dunninald* (Coupar Angus, 1999)

Statistical Accounts of Scotland (First and *Second),* available online at http://edina.ac.uk/stat-acc-scot

Stephens, H., *The Book of the Farm* (London, 1844)

SWRI (Taynuilt), *Taynuilt: Our History* (pamphlet) (Oban,1967)

Taylor, H. P., *A Shetland Parish Doctor* (Lerwick, 1948)

Train, J., *History of the Buchanites* (Irvine, 1883)

Index

218   *Index*